MIKE BONIFER & JESSIE SHTERNSHUS

CT
SHIᕼI

50 GAMES FOR
50 ****ING DAYS
LIKE TODAY

ILLUSTRATIONS BY JIM WARD

Contact us at
www.ctrlshift.biz

ASTER ✱✱✱✱

How's your ****ing day?

What word do these four **** represent to you? How did you read them when you saw the title of the book? Chances are, you inserted a profanity. That's what traditional journalism uses asterisks for. But traditional journalism is an artifact of the past. Are there any words that cannot be spelled out in all their profane glory anymore?

Well then, for ****'s sake, let's play a different game. Let's say the four asterisks can conceal any word at all, whether it has four letters or not. Now, what word do the asterisks represent? Make it creative. Distinctive. Your own. That's what happens when you play with the type of day you're having. You are creative about it in order to make it your own.

So how's your ****ing day? Could be a 'Finding' kind of day. Could be a 'Killer' day. Could be a 'Loving' day or a 'Sad' day. Could be an 'I Really Don't Feel Like Talking About It Can We Wait Until Later In The Week?' day.

Characterizing a day is a way of *CTRLing* your response to it. When things *Shift*, *CTRL* over your response gives you the ability to navigate and make sense of the change. When things are inert, nothing seems to be happening. If you want to put some life into your scene, your response can do that, too. We respond differently to different kinds of days and rightfully so. You don't wear your parka in a heatwave and you don't host a party on the arrival of bad news. Or maybe you do. Your response is up to you. There are ways of responding to the type of day you're having that are better and more likely to be effective than others. That is what this book is meant to provide.

The Games are structured ways of responding to different kinds of days. Each game gives you a way to *CTRL Shift*.

SHIFT

What is *Shift?*

Shift is a Fierce Flow of Events. It is the world made visible and experienced in unprecedented ways. We can communicate and connect in dimensions and at speeds heretofore unknown in human history. Or maybe we've forgotten these things as a species and we're experiencing them on a generational level. Either way, we are becoming conscious as if for the first time of our changing work and lifestyle environments. That's fierce.

Shift is the Unexpectedness of Everything. The flow of events in the networked world is continuous and volatile. There's no script for it or formula for dealing with it. The events that affected us yesterday are different from those that affect us today. Every moment is a new moment. We can know *Shift* is happening, yet how it happens is very often a surprise.

Shift is "What if?" and "Never mind" having babies. In times of *Shift*, "what if" can be a powerful way of exploring the possibilities. "Never mind" is the understanding that no particular future that we've imagined is guaranteed.

Shift is a Way of Life. The evolving environment in which we live and work demands that we evolve with it or risk being made obsolete by it. This statement has always been true. It has never been more dramatic than it is today, if for no other reason than today, it's about us.

Shift is A Thrill Ride. Remember when we were children and almost every experience was thrilling because it was brand-new? Our instinct was to enjoy these experiences. They were markers of our growth. The wild rides we're on today are also markers of our growth.

CTRL

What is *CTRL*?

CTRL is Response to Change. ****ing Days Like These are rife with both pitfalls and opportunities. Skilled players see pitfalls far enough in advance to avoid most of them (no one avoids them all). They also see opportunities early (no one sees them all) and act on them decisively.

CTRL is Perspective. Where one person sees a roadblock, another sees an alternate path. This is perspective. It is vital to *CTRLing Shift.* The view out your window might be the same as yesterday; the way you're responding to it doesn't have to be.

CTRL is Opportunity Seen. All changes reveal opportunity that was not present before the change transpired. Let the *Shift* hit the fan and let your new situation guide you to opportunities you couldn't see before.

CTRL is Work. What works today might not work tomorrow. Don't allow yourself to become complacent.

Keep questioning everything. This keeps things new and fresh and helps you maintain *CTRL* when *Shift* happens.

CTRL is Imagination. Let's face it, if you cannot imagine a story with a favorable ending, you are at the absolute mercy of your environment, like a cork on the ocean. The cork is not the story; the ocean is the story and you are subject to its whims. When you respond with imagination, you're like a bird on the ocean. You are in a relationship with your environment. You can respond to the changing waves. You have options. You and the ocean are co-creating a story.

CTRL is Focus. The ability to hold your focus in a world of constant distractions is vital for keeping cool and making good decisions. This book will help you with that.

CTRL is Participation. There is no better way of persuading people to join you on your quest than by your authentic participation in a narrative that matters to them, too. When we participate, we gain empathy and understanding that help us adapt to whatever kind of *Shift* a ****ing Day may bring.

CTRL is Favorable Odds. We don't live in a world of certainties. The *CTRL* we have depends on our ability to nudge our odds in a consistently favorable direction. Playing the Games in this book will improve your odds on ****ing Days Like Today.

CTRL is Presence. Don't give your attention to what you think should happen. Give it to what is happening.

GAME

What is a *Game*?

There are many definitions for what constitutes a game. Sports definitions. Casino definitions. MMORPGs and ARGs and RPGs and all manner of gamifications put to all types of uses. There are power games, head games, world domination games, money games and children's games. There are playful games and serious games. Secret games and transparent ones. There are games within games. Games played for the benefit of individuals and games played by entire populations.

Our definition: "*A game is an agreed-upon structure for play that produces beneficial outcomes.*"

A game provides a point of focus for interacting with your environment and the people in it. This book is a starter set: 50 Games that will help you hack 50 types of *Shift*. When your environment *Shifts*, either for better or worse, your focus on a game will help you adapt to the change and tilt the odds toward favorable outcomes for yourself and the people with whom you share the day.

Here are three important concepts to understand about games:

1. There is always a game. A game can be a 'Big G' high stakes game with lots of livelihoods and futures at stake, as in Bill and Melinda Gates' "End Malaria" game. Or it can be a low-stakes 'little g' game, as in a "Where Will We Eat Lunch?" game. Even low-stakes games can have big consequences. We have a friend, Michele, who as the new head of an existing product team for a media company, spent six months playing what she calls *The New Kid in School* game. This helped her learn a lot more and get way more done than if she'd begun her reign with, let's say, a *New Sheriff in Town* game. Not all games are created equal and no two games are alike. Even slightly different games can produce radically different outcomes.

Especially when it comes to matters of love, money and power, games are often deep and can be tragically unfair to their players.

It is possible to see and deal with the differences between good and bad games, between productive and unproductive ones. Visible and hidden ones. Win/Win, Win/Lose and Lose/Lose games. However visible they may be to their players or how fair the outcomes are, *there is always a game.*

2. *There are infinite games.* The 50 Games described in this book are like 50 grains of sand in a hundred Saharas when it comes to how many games are possible. Let them inspire your own variations. Share them. In playing together, we see and experience see the world in new ways. New possibilities emerge. Our ability to play mirrors our capacity for growth—it's limitless.

3. *Games are infinite.* Not only are there infinite games, there are infinite possibilities in any given game. Because a game offers infinite possibilities for positive outcomes, it is a much better way of approaching your day than, let's say, a strategy with only one desirable outcome. If your only objective for the day is to get a raise and you don't get the raise, you'll probably consider that day a failure.

The point of a game is to focus on it so as to discover its possibilities. That's what we're giving you the means to do. Games are a playful way of relating to one's environment and fellow players and getting unique and valuable outcomes, each and every time.

Your ability to *CTRL Shift* with these games comes down to questions like:

When confronted with a *Shifty* Day, can you spin it in a productive direction?

When good fortune comes your way, how can you share it most effectively?

How much game do you have?

If you're playing a bad game, how do you change it?

If you've got a good and productive game, how do you play it even better?

NAME YOUR ****ING DAY, PLAY YOUR ****ING GAME

In a world of infinite possibilities, many beginnings are valid, so don't make a big deal out of naming your ****ing Day. Keep it easy. Simple. Sort through the list of ****ing Days and find a day that sounds like the kind of day you're having or expect to have.

Then, put that ****ing Day's game into play, at whatever scale and tempo works for you. The important thing is to be persistent with it throughout the day, to be aware at all times of opportunities to play your game.

Note that some games are designed for individuals and others for small groups, such as a team of co-workers. Some will work for both individuals and groups.

Remember that even when you're on your own, you're never alone. It is always possible to connect with other people, with your environment, with your deeper self. A game will help you do this. Think of this book as a portal to a world with many more possibilities than you imagine you have for any given day. They are there, waiting for you to discover them. If you are anticipating a particular type of day, or if you're already in the thick of it, if you're having the kind of day you want to change, or the kind of day you want to get more out of, you'll find this book helpful. The book is a set of keys. How you use them, what they open, and where those doorways lead will be up to you.

****ING DAYS LIKE TODAY

A DAY OF WINE AND ROSES

This is a day you fall in love. It could be with anyone or anything, for any reason. So, it could be a new romance. Or maybe you're in love with your new boss (in a totally workplace appropriate way, of course). Maybe it's a new technology, a movie, a quote, a meme or some other piece of spreadable content. You love your new business partner. Your new team. Your city. Your home. Your life. Your new shoes. Whatever it is, you have cause to celebrate because this is love. The fuzzy wuzzies, the oh doctors, the bang bang boogie, the "don't stop!"

Here is a totally workplace appropriate way to hack whatever floats your Love Boat on a day like today.

GAME OF THE DAY
SECRET ADMIRER

Today you are…(cue theme music)…*Secret Admirer.*

Secret Admirer moves through the day by expressing appreciation for everyone and everything, *in the most secretive way possible*. On a day like today, it's perfectly fine for you to talk behind people's backs, because you're going to give them rave reviews. On a day like today, your responsibility is to make others feel good about themselves, ideally without them even knowing why. It's you. You're responsible. Yet no one knows. Such is the life of a superhero like Secret Admirer.

Secret Admirer gives invisible gifts. Opens doors. Smiles. Nods. Acknowledges. Secret Admirer's spirit is one of generosity. Secret Admirer's sidekick is Gratitude. Secret Admirer sheds the everyday spectacles of ego and judgment in order to generate laser vision on the environment and the people in it. Secret Admirer pays attention and respect.

To Secret Admirer, everyone and everything matters. Secret Admirer's world does not consist solely of, nor is it affected exclusively by, human beings. Plants, objects, animals, art, weather—all of it has life and all of is susceptible to Secret Admirer's superhuman gifts of secret admiration.

Here's the main guideline for the game: you can't let anyone know. Don't get found out. The "keeping it secret" aspect of the game is part of the fun. How much admiration can you express without anyone realizing it's your game?

WARNING #1: Do not confuse *Secret Admirer* with the clichéd and tiresome game of *Kissing Ass*, which needs visibility to be effective. The person whose ass you're kissing needs to know it's you doing the kissing, which means it's obvious to other people, so don't kid yourself about that. *Secret Admirer* is a much better game, because it plays out in many dimensions. It stimulates conversation. It gives you the thrill of keeping secrets without any of the harmful side effects.

WARNING #2: This is not personal infatuation. Secret Admirer has a love interest, but that's a different ****ing Game for a different ****ing Day.

How many ways can you express your admiration secretly today? This is your challenge. A note on a whiteboard. A compliment to a co-worker. A cup of water for a thirsty plant. A smile for a service worker. A Post-It on a coffee pot for the person who made the coffee. Buying a coffee for the next person in line. Stealth kindness is the best kind because it pays itself ahead in ways you don't even have to worry about. Don't forget to disguise your handwriting!

And if you get found out, own it. Fess up to the instance without giving away the game. It was an accident. A flaw in your otherwise curmudgeonly armor. You don't have to reveal that secret admiring is your superpower for the day.

THE DAY YOU NEED A TUNE-UP

Your team has been missing deadlines. Your sprints feel more like forced marches. Every request gets met with grumbling, hemming and hawing, like an engine that's not running right.

Teams need service just like a car does. Today's the day you bring your team in for servicing.

You need to get your brakes looked at, because your stops tend to be rolling stops. Grinding stops. You often have to pump the brakes several times to get a response. How can you get everyone working at the same tempo?

You need to change your oil, because there's too much friction and overheating poses a threat to performance. When tempers flare, jealousies simmer or discontent boils over, you're not in for a very enjoyable trip.

With the many demands made on it, your team can find itself going many different directions at once. You may need to get your steering adjusted.

It's the kind of day when you may get better mileage if you spend it being of service to your team. Here's one way to do that.

GAME OF THE DAY
ANTIDOTE

One of the most toxic phrases in your vocabulary is "Yes, but..." It's a slow-acting toxin; odorless, tasteless, its effects perhaps unnoticed at first, its presence masked by the flavor of positivity or by whatever conversation you inject it into. You or anyone who uses the phrase "Yes but" can develop a reputation as a realist, a pragmatist or a perfectionist, when in fact what you're doing is drugging everyone on your team with the arsenic of adversarialism. And then, little by little, here's what happens:

The discussion sloooows doooowwwwn. Doubt creeps into flow and begins damming it into pools of indecision. Control begins exerting itself in the form of self-imposed and other-imposed judgment and self-consciousness. Negativity throws shade at hope. Creative notions get smothered in their infancy by criticism. Intuition gets dampened by rationality. You grow lackadaisical. The glimmer in your co-workers' eyes begins to fade. Speech gets dulled by imprecision. "Yes but" derails ideas and kills momentum. Its venom is slow-acting and deadly.

If every idea got bit by the venomous "Yes but," no breakthroughs would ever come to life. We'd never see the rose for the thorns. Yes, the rose is lovely, *but* those thorns can draw blood. Yes, a horse is a totally fabulous animal, *but* people get hurt when they fall off them. The "Yes but" way to make sure you never fall off is to never ride a horse.

Hack this poison today!

Begin your game by noticing how many times you and others hear the phrase "Yes but" in conversations meant to move a project, a process or a mind into new space. Begin replacing the "but" with the word "and." The operative phrase is "Yes and." Do this first as a mental exercise, to sharpen your *heeding practice*: your skill at observing, listening and paying attention to the subtle cues of language. And then begin doing it aloud in conversations, consciously replacing the word "but" with "and" as often as possible. "Yes and" is the *Antidote* to the poison of "Yes but."

See how using "and" will propel ideas, build on them and keep your team engaged and onboard.

Yes, the rose is lovely *and* the thorns are a counterpoint to its loveliness. A hint of danger makes a thing more alluring.

Yes, a horse is a fabulous animal *and* you'll be fabulous, too, when you learn to ride. It is a test of character whether you get back on a horse that has thrown you. Everyone falls. Even best riders fall. Ask someone who rides better than you why you fell. Analysis of performance is a key to improvement.

The poison of "Yes but" will get you nowhere. The *Antidote* of "Yes and" opens the door to a universe of possibilities.

ORIENTATION DAY

You find yourself in a completely new environment, surrounded by alien life forms with strange cultures. Your familiar *CTRLs*, the ones you have always counted on to orient you and navigate the currents of change, are no good on this planet.

A day like this does not call for the kinds of subtle adjustments you might make when there's been a normal and predictable transition from one day to the next. No, this day is different from the day before in almost every way you can imagine.

You're a newbie. An experiment. People speak and dress differently in this place. Their customs are different. Their value system, unfathomable. You are a non-native expected to honor the local customs and speak the local language. It is a sudden and complete immersion in an unfamiliar context. It is a shock to the system.

In terms of business, this is the day you get introduced to your new team. The first day you're on your own in in a new territory. The day you pivot as a company to re-define your brand's market approach.

During the Dotcom era of the late 1990s, we worked on an internet project in Tokyo for an old-line Japanese firm with 2,000+ employees that had been taken over by a U.S. company after a major scandal had destroyed the Japanese market's trust in the old-line firm. When the new (non-Asian) president arrived in Tokyo, his first meeting was with the outgoing president, who had been badly tarnished by the scandal. The outgoing president, as customary, offered his business card to the incoming person with two hands and a slight bow. The new president held up his hand and refused the business card with a statement that may have never been uttered before on Japanese soil: "Oh no, we're not going to do that business card bullshit."

We can tell you that as this story circulated inside the organization, its employees initiated another game, whose objective was to negate whatever the new president had in mind. This game was so deep, it was invisible to all but the employees of the old Japanese company. The entire game was embedded in that one line of code, "We're not going to do that business card bullshit." We only knew the game existed because it was explained to us by one employee, a woman who liked to have a Marlboro and a beer after work. It was like something out of a William Gibson novel. The shadow game was deeper, more complex, with infinitely more possible moves. Within a year, the new guy was out, replaced by a Japanese woman who has since restored the company to prominence in the Asian market under a new brand name.

The new president did not, as it turned out, have a very good game for his Orientation Day at his new company. He forgot that he was the new kid in school. A stage hand asked to play leading role.

Here's a better game.

GAME OF THE DAY
GAP CONVERSATION

A *Gap Conversation* is a great exercise for seeding conversations and developing cross-gap communication. Here's how to play: Pair up with someone and put a conversation gap between you. For example, pretend that the other person is from 100 years in the past. Now explain a modern-day object to her, i.e. a mobile device, a computer or salt lamp. Do your best to explain how the object works and why she might see value in having one. You can even try to sell it to her.

We get in the habit of taking ourselves and our own awareness of the world around us for granted. We make assumptions that other people must know what we know, especially if we are in the same line of work or we are similar in age and experience. Yet there's always a gap. No one else knows exactly what we know, nor have they learned about the world in the same way. As the improv teacher, Dave Razowsky, says, "How can someone know what you know if they haven't been where you've been?"

This game gives us practice in, first, recognizing such gaps and second, closing those gaps. In reality, the gaps between us may be so small as to be barely discernible. We are, after all, close to people, connected to them in many ways. One of the benefits of the game is that it makes the gaps big. Aiming at a large target starts the practice that will lead, eventually, to aiming at the bullseye. *Gap Conversations* give you a large target. Having practiced, you'll begin to draw a better bead on the small differences and misunderstandings that impede good communication.

Here are more examples of *Gap Conversations*. You and your partner can take turns at being the Explainer and the Explainee:

- Explain the moon to a child.
- Explain an airplane to an aborigine.
- Describe email to a telephone operator from the 1930s.
- Explain a cat to a dog.
- Explain Instagram to a grandparent.

Everyone speaks a different language. Accepting that these gaps exist and working to bridge them is a much better game than seeing the gaps as a failure to communicate. The failures to communicate happen because we don't acknowledge the gaps and act on them.

This game helps you develop a universal way to get people to understand each other. It helps you develop an appreciation for ideas, objects, people and environments that you might otherwise take for granted. This game will help you work on skills you need when the gaps are smaller, more nuanced, perhaps not even visible to the people creating them. Closing the small gaps can be the difference between moving your story forward or seeing it get derailed by gaps that widen into disagreements, instead of creating consensus.

THE DAY YOU'RE STUCK

It's a sticky, stuck, sucky kind of day. You can't pull a paper cup from a drink dispenser without it sticking. A paper clip you've been bending back and forth for five minutes breaks, whereupon you stick yourself and draw blood. Stuck. Bloody stuck!

You stare at a whiteboard for a very long time before you finally uncap a marker, draw three intersecting circles, put a tiny question mark in the spot where all three overlap, re-cap the marker and take an early lunch.

Your code keeps crashing and you don't know why.

Your boss sends you a link to a petaflop of data with an email that says "Make sense of this."

It's the kind of day you get cornered by two co-workers who want to talk to you about the appropriateness of their outside-work relationship.

This is not the kind of relationship you thought you'd be in at this stage in your life. This is not what you went to school for. The guy ahead of you in line for promotion isn't going anywhere. You're not making a difference. Not contributing.

Where do you see yourself in five years? On a day like today, probably right where you are, doing the same damn thing you're doing today. You're on a treadmill and the scenery does not change.

It's the kind of day that makes you think, for the first time in years, about that time when you were five years old and got accidentally locked inside your grandma's basement with the cockatoo that wouldn't shut up. You're feeling trapped and panicky, just like you did in Grandma's basement with the cockatoo.

Fortunately, that was then, this is now. Today, you have lots of possibilities for getting unstuck, beginning with this game.

GAME OF THE DAY
ACRONYMS

Sometimes we get stuck because we think there's only one way to get a job done, only one way of describing things, and we don't question the status quo. This is an exercise in *Shifting* consciously when the status quo has seized hold of your life or work.

Our friend, Wanda, is a director of student counseling at an online university. When her school's administrators saddled her team with an app designed to automate student interactions, she and her team composed a song they'd sing about the app whenever it was adversely affecting their performance, which was all the time. This was much more alarming to the administrators than if Wanda and her team had groused about the app through the chain of command channels. The admins abandoned the app within a semester.

CTRLing Shift can be something as simple as changing the way we think about office jargon to get us out of the "stuck" mode and into a flow mode. Most workplaces are heavy with acronyms. In fact, most of life is full of acronyms (YOLO, y'know?). Think of the acronyms that accompany you every day. We're going to play with those.

Make a list of all the acronyms used at your current job or in your day-to-day life. Go through each one and decide on something different that each letter in the acronym can stand for. If you'd like to add more acronyms to your list or need prompts to get you started, you can refer to an Acronym Dictionary online. OMG, you may be surprised, or maybe not, by how much we all, no matter what kind of work we do, from CPA to NASA scientist, rely on jargon to SWAG our way through a day.

Here are some familiar acronyms and how you might use them to hack the *Acronyms* game:

YOLO: Yesterday's Obligations Look Odd

ROFLMAO: Really Offensive Family Littering Mausoleum After Obituary

SWOT: Smells Wafting Over Tarpits

WYSIWYG: When You Suck It Worries Your Grandma

ASAP: Always Southern Always Proud

LUCKY DAY

Things are clicking. The world is Macaroni and you are the Cheese.

On a day like today, cars pull out of parking spaces for you, as if their drivers had been waiting for you to arrive.

The client calls to postpone your presentation two minutes before you were going to ask for an extension. Your flight is delayed an hour and your connecting flight is late arriving by (you're not going to believe what happens!) *exactly one hour*!

Your significant other calls you at work to say he loves you. There is no apparent agenda beyond that.

The thing you lost that one time and had pretty much given up on ever finding? Today's the day you find it.

On a day like today, good fortune can and will take many forms. The point is to notice. To be aware and be grateful.

Only two kinds of days involve luck. Lucky days and days when we don't realize how lucky we are. There's no such thing as "bad lucky" or "good lucky." There's lucky. A lucky day is a good day.

GAME OF THE DAY
THIS IS YOUR LUCKY DAY

On a day like today, with you being so lucky and all, you've got plenty of luck to go around. Your obligation is to share your luck and make other people's days lucky, too.

All you need to play the game is the phrase *This is Your Lucky Day.* The objective of the game is to put these words into action as many times as possible.

There are four guidelines to the game:

1. The phrase cannot be delivered ironically. You cannot tell someone who just got a parking ticket "This is your lucky day" and have it count toward your total for the day, unless you pay the ticket.

2. The phrase cannot be used as a pickup line.

3. The phrase must be accompanied by action. The action must be spontaneous. Don't script. Instead, prepare. Be on the lookout for opportunities to bring "luck" to someone, whatever form that takes in the moment.

4. The phrase does not have to be spoken aloud. Give yourself a one point bonus each time you do (and don't come off as a douche), but you can still score if you simply create someone's lucky moment while saying the words to yourself.

It is a good reminder that luck is a baby born to preparation and opportunity. Our best luck rewards more than just ourselves. It's impossible to share without giving up something of ourselves. In this instance, we share our attention and our luck. We give less of these to ourselves and more of them to those around us. We send luck on its merry way, confident that it'll visit us again someday.

THE DAY YOU CAN'T BE SERIOUS

You and your boss are in different dimensions of space-time, because the demands being made on you and your team cannot possibly be met in the time and space you've been given.

You have a goal for your team of checking off 15 open tasks per day and you've been handed an assignment with 300 open tasks and more on the way. You have nowhere near enough time or support to check them all off by your ship date. You are are in a position where you are going to piss off at least some people, maybe everybody.

On a day like today, you're stuck putting out fires at work, when you promised your son you'd be at his school's talent show and your spouse thought you'd be home in time for dinner. You have a parent down in Louisiana with health issues and your siblings are waiting to hear from you (and by hearing from you, they mean sending money). The 'Check Engine' light in your car has been red for a disturbingly long time.

You have an urgent need for information from a co-worker who has gone Area 51 on your ass and is nowhere to be found.

A co-worker ruins your lunch by talking about folic acid the entire time. And she's not even sitting at your table. She's just loud. She can't be serious, can she?

Is there any real reward for taking on an impossible assignment or is it a fool's errand? Can days like this resolve happily or is that only in Julia Roberts movies and Broadway musicals? This game will help you find answers to one of life's great paradoxes:

How can people expect you to take them and their batshit situations seriously? Seriously...

GAME OF THE DAY
TEAR IT DOWN, BUILD IT UP

Think of an existing, well-established product, such as an airplane, a lawn mower, a fork, toilet paper. Anything familiar and in common use. Write the name of the item at the top of a flip chart. Divide into groups and take eight minutes to brainstorm. Provide a description of the item as if it were a brand new product and get the group to come up with as many reasons as possible why this product will *never* succeed. Groups should write all the reasons down on the flip chart paper and then each group will present all the reasons why this product is so bad.

After both groups have shared all their reasons, talk about what benefits there are to re-looking at a product for flaws in order to improve it. Talk about how we often accept things the way they are, especially if they are working sufficiently. It is important to look at things from a new perspective. You may discover a new idea by looking at a familiar product in a new way.

Okay, let's keep going. Now, take the same product you've shredded and go in the other direction with it. Build it up. Praise its attributes. List all the things that make it great, useful or indispensable. Which list is longer, the faults list or the attributes list?

Often, we are more adept at finding faults than we are at identifying positive traits. It's as true of people as it is of things, if not more so. (If you're feeling adventurous, you can repeat the exercise using yourself as the "product." Check your ego and go for it!)

Here's another thing about this game: you can see how many "why not" reasons you are capable of listing for products that have obviously been successful. Every successful venture must run a gauntlet of subjective opinions before it reaches the marketplace and broad acceptance. This game demonstrates that the difference between successful and unsuccessful ventures is often determined by the way we see the world.

Do you get sidetracked, discouraged or derailed by the "Yes buts" and negative opinions of people who fixate on "what's wrong?" Or is your vision strong, clear and persistent enough to stay focused on what's good and helpful about your work and, more importantly, about the people in your lives?

CLEANING DAY

You have too much clutter in your office, your job, your life. It's time to clean it all up and put things in order. Time to toss that which is not needed so you can be more focused and attentive to what is most important.

You have been so busy building, testing, debugging and patching that your tools are scattered and leftover pieces of your work muck up your space like week-old guacamole in an office refrigerator.

Like every human, your success is dependent on your ability to recognize and work with patterns. When there's too much clutter, clutter is the only pattern you can see. When you hit the point where there's more noise than signal in your process, it's time for a day like this one. Eliminating noise will have the same effect as boosting your signal. You will be more clearly heard and understood and, as a result, you'll be more effective in everything you do.

Clutter gets in the way of creativity. In fact, it's often the only thing that gets in the way. Creativity wants to happen and will happen, as long as you remove that clutter.

This game will help you eliminate noise and improve your focus. Historical narratives are like cobwebs. Sweep them aside so you can see the future clearly. Rumors are like cockroaches. Kill them before they breed. Your judgment junks up your process. Stick it in your attic and save it for your grandchildren.

Here's your broom. Get busy!

GAME OF THE DAY
SMOG

First, brainstorm a list of 20 tasks you need to get done.

For each of these tasks, assign a SMOG: Describe the *Situation*, your *Motivation* in performing the task, the expected *Outcome* from performing the task and the *Gallows*, which is the price you'll pay if the task doesn't get done. Make each task immediate, as if it were the very next thing on your list of to-do's. Keep them in the present tense:

Situation: When _____ is happening

Motivation: I want to _____

Outcome: So I can _____ .

Gallows: If it doesn't happen, _____ will be the price we pay.

When you have done this for the 20 (or however many) tasks that are cluttering your headspace, prioritize each of the SMOGs:

1s are the most urgent. The Situation affects more people; your Motivation is high; the Outcome is compelling; if you don't do it, you're headed to the Gallows (and there will be no humor about it).

2s are middle ground. Outcomes may be a little less certain. You may survive if you don't complete the task (though maybe not for much longer).

3s can wait. They don't affect as many people. You're not as personally engaged in the scenario. Perhaps it's not on anyone's radar at the moment.

Quickly total your scores. The five lowest scores are the tasks you're going to tackle today and the SMOG will start to clear. If a new task gets handed to you during the day, quickly rank it. If it falls within the five most urgent SMOGs, add it to your list and drop #5. You can only do so much in a day and this game will help you synthesize what is do-able, helpful and urgent.

THE DAY YOU LEAVE HOME

We have all experienced it. The place that sustained your growth for most of your life can't sustain it anymore. Whatever and wherever you call home, it is time to let go and leave.

Leaving home can mean reducing your reliance on a mentor or counselor who has watched over and protected you as you made and learned from your early mistakes.

It can mean moving from your first employer out of college to a new situation or leaving a team that has become like family to you to seek out fresh challenges elsewhere.

Or it can mean, you know, leaving home, moving out of the house and declaring your independence.

Leaving home isn't always an easy decision. There are lots of comforts typically associated with home. You are cushioned from the harsher realities. Routines and people are predictable.

Here's why leaving home is an important day of change: your discomfort is vital to your growth. Unless you are willing to throw yourself into unfamiliar surroundings and situations, you'll never learn. And if you never learn, you'll never grow.

Woolie Reithermann was a great Disney animator and producer of films, such as *Jungle Book* and *The Rescuers* for Disney, and also quite an adventurer. When he was in his teens, he and his brother built and flew their own airplane. An avid surfer, he once said to us, "Before you can surf, you have to let the waves toss you around until you can understand how a wave works." This is the way of the world. Before you can learn anything, you need to get out of your comfort zone. This necessitates leaving home, the place where you are most secure, and entering a world where there are no guarantees, where you'll of necessity grow and learn or shrink from the challenges facing you. One thing's certain: nothing will be as it was before you left home.

Remember, just because you are putting down new roots, it doesn't mean the old roots aren't lasting and deep. Home will always be where the heart is.

Now get going. Go. Be on your way. And don't forget to write!

GAME OF THE DAY
MOON LANDING

What could be more about leaving home than an astronaut leaving the earth's orbit to visit the moon? Imagine what Neil Armstrong, Buzz Aldrin and Michael Collins felt on their Apollo 11 mission to the moon. No human beings had ever been farther from home or left home in such a visible and dramatic fashion.

We'll model today's game on their mission.

Today is your day to take a small step for [garbled transmission] man, one giant leap for mankind.

First, you must practice. Before Apollo 11 could launch and land its astronauts on the moon, they had to practice. From CNN.com:

> "In January 1963, Neil Armstrong and four other Apollo astronauts took a field trip to Arizona's Meteor Crater and Sunset Crater, a dormant volcano. Geologists then briefed the astronauts on how those Earthly landscapes were similar to what they might encounter on the moon.

> "In the years that followed, Apollo 11 crew members also toured the Grand Canyon and spent time testing lunar rovers at Bonito Crater northeast of Flagstaff, where the rough, rocky surface mimicked what some geologists thought would exist on the moon.

"Geologists flew over Sunset Crater and other landforms in Cessna 182s, taking aerial photos, so the astronauts might better understand the lunar geology they were likely to see."

Note that there are three kinds of speed you'll have to monitor as part of your Moon Landing: *Escape Velocity*, *Cruising Speed* and *Landing Speed*.

Rather than measure your speed by the clock, which is not yours to *CTRL*, we want you to measure it by your tempo, which is within your *CTRL*. Each kind of speed has a tempo associated with it.

For Escape Velocity, you are going to do things quickly, in rapid tempo. In music, this is known as *Allegro*. What happens when the pace is that fast? What do you have to monitor? Are others moving at your tempo? What could slow you down? Anything that slows you down will diminish your tempo and if you don't have fast tempo, you may never get the day off the ground. If you don't increase your tempo, your orbit will likely be the same one you were in yesterday. You'll be going in circles. Escape Velocity ensures an upward and onward spiral.

Once you achieve Cruising Speed, you are going to be more laid back and take in all the newness of your environment. You're going to enjoy the view. You will gain perspective as, having escaped your old orbit and the habits associated with it, you see your old place as less significant and smaller and your destination as ever closer, larger and gaining definition.

For Landing Speed, recognize what it is like to touch down and plant your feet on new ground. What bumps do you hit? Will there be craters in the way of your landing?

Chart your three tempos for this day like an astronaut mapping a trip to the moon or a musician imagining a composition. Then drop the beat and take one giant step. (It was 3.5 feet when Neil Armstrong took it. Watch your step. You're going to bounce a bit.)

MEET-AND-GREET DAY

You are headed for a first-time visit to one of your company's many locations. You walk in and you meet your contact at the location, let's say his name is Hoon Koo (coincidentally the same name as a friend of ours). He walks you around the awesomely-designed office space, introducing you to people. You meet Brent, Kim Su, Sara and Krisha from a project team. And then Erik, Fleenoil, Simo, Daniela and Caitlin in Customer Service. Down the hall, you run into Gabe, another Sara, Evie and Everett from Legal. In five minutes, you have met 24 people and the only name you remember is Sara. You know there are two of them, but you don't remember which two, and if you did, you wouldn't remember which Sara is which. Their names have left the building. You're left feeling like a stranger in a foreign land, who does not speak the language. All you can do, it seems, is embarrass yourself throughout the rest of the two days you'll be in that location by asking people to whom you've been introduced what their names are.

How many times do we find ourselves meeting new people and not remembering their names? A new environment with a new cast of characters contains so much information, we can get overwhelmed by it all and lose our focus.

Here's a dose of help in the form of a game.

GAME OF THE DAY
VAMPIRE GEORGE CLOONEY

In his book, *Moonwalking with Einstein*, Joshua Foer, who had an unexceptional memory, chronicles his experience training his memory, using tried and true techniques practiced by memory masters since the days of the Greeks, and becoming the U.S. memorization champion. This game will give you several ways to improve your memory and retention of new information and associate the names with the faces of people you're meeting for the first time.

Today, you'll be making up appropriate nicknames and anagrams for the people whose names you'd like to remember. It will give you a way to associate names with faces. Think of it as your own internal facial recognition algorithm.

The key to a mnemonic device is to associate the new name or object with something or someone familiar that's already lodged firmly in your memory. One convenient way to do this with people you're meeting for the first time is to associate them with well-known celebrities.

Say you get introduced to a man named George, who's in his forties with salt and pepper hair. In your mind, you could associate him with George Clooney, for whom your brain has already stored tens or hundreds of thousands of impressions. Let's say that George's last name is Bloodgood. You have an image of George Clooney drinking blood. Vampire George Clooney is the image triggered whenever you see George Bloodgood. With that picture in your mind, how could you ever forget George Bloodgood?

It takes practice. If you've never done this before, don't expect to perfect your process today. With practice, though, you'll be able to literally make these associations at the speed of thought, because the associations are already stored in your memory. The practice involves accessing them quickly and associating the visuals in your memory with the visual of the person's face.

Let's do it again. One of the people on the new team is a social media strategist named Ronni Phillips. She has red hair, so you associate her with Ronald McDonald. In your associative memory, Ronald McDonald is fixing the milk shake machine with a Phillips head screwdriver. This is the image you'll trigger whenever you see Ronni Phillips: Ronald McDonald fixing a milk shake machine with a Phillips head screwdriver. It's all already there. All you've got to do is make the associations. You can get superfast at this. All it takes is practice.

Let's say your "Meet-and-Greet Day" includes a scene where you meet the Board of Directors of your company. This is a major day for you because they are considering your project and you do not want to screw up anyone's name. You've studied their photos online and think you have their names and faces memorized, but when you enter the board room, you realize to your horror that all their official photos were taken when Ronald Reagan was president.

Let's say your memory game is rhymes. Miriam borders on Delirium. Paul is built like a Wall. Sandy's hair looks like Cotton Candy. Marcellus has been to four Coachellas, and Stan goes to Burning Man.

There's another mnemonic device that'll help you game a day like today. It's what's commonly known (and Foer describes in detail in his book) as a "memory palace." This is a place you've memorized because it is known and familiar to you, such as a family home, a school or a workplace where you spend lots of time. As you encounter lists and people whose names you feel you ought to remember, you can "park" them in different places in your memory palace.

Let's say your "Meet-and-Greet Day" includes memorizing a list of features for your new cloud product. There are 20 of them and you'll be quizzed on them at the next sales meeting.

You can use a memory palace to help you remember the product features.

Say you spent a lot of time in a particular park when you were a child and it's as vivid as anyplace in your memory, because it matters to you. This place is filled with positive associations and details such as smells, sounds and textures. This is going to be your memory palace. It's where you'll "place" the product feature set.

You are going to 'take a walk' through your memory palace and, along your path, you are going to stash the 20 features of your cloud product. For example, one of your product features is voice voting. You remember the place in the park where you and your friends would play the game of Red Rover and vote with your voices about who should "come over." This is where you will 'stash' voice voting, in the perpetual game of Red Rover going on in the park that will become your memory palace.

If another feature is e-commerce, that's the ice cream truck. If another is a mobile security layer, this was where all the parents sat. In your memory palace, the mobile security feature "clings" to the clinging parents. And so it goes. After you have deposited all 20 product features in your memory palace, recalling them is a matter of taking a familiar walk through a familiar place and recalling all the associations you've made with that place. The brand new associations will naturally and, with practice, cluster with the old.

A Foggy Day

Inconsistent decision-making and poor understanding of objectives will lose a team in a hurry. It may reach the point where no one knows anything. Everything is guesswork. Opinion. Arbitrary. Without any apparent rhyme or reason.

By contrast, if decision-making is aligned and objectives are well-defined, everyone on the team can perform at a high level. The right questions get posed and there's a shared feeling that everyone's work points toward a solution to a problem or the completion of a task.

Your role on a day like today is to create clarity. Decide! Explain! Teach! Make sense of things! If your team is lost and adrift, as in a fog, your role is to be the lighthouse that will help them get their bearings and avoid a shipwreck. When your team is getting tossed and turned like a ship in a storm, your role is to provide the steady steering that will see them through to port.

Imagine if the crew of a ship caught in a storm got the kind of clarity from its leadership that teams get from leaders with poor decision-making skills:

"We need more research before we choose a direction."

"Let's compile a database and let a history of past routes determine our course."

"Do the best you can. I'll be in the lifeboat if you need me."

That's not you. Not today. Here's a way to help clear that fog.

GAME OF THE DAY
THREE THINGS CLEAR

If there are three areas of confusion on a day like today, you need a game that addresses those three areas and, wouldn't you know, that's exactly what we've got for you. We even named it clearly. We could've named this same game *Trilateral Commission*, but that would only add to the plague of vague that's already got you in its grip. Hence, *Three Things Clear*.

From every encounter you have, you will seek to get *Three Things Clear*: 1) the directions or instructions; 2) what the hell you're doing; 3) what the hell everybody else is doing.

In every scene you're in today, however brief it is, give yourself a point each time you get one thing clear, until you have at least three points. Only then can you move to your next scene.

Say you're meeting a customer for breakfast to discuss new business. Be clear about what you want for breakfast:

"Oatmeal, brown sugar, strawberries, no bananas, no raisins, skim milk, black coffee, raw sugar, a water, no ice."

And then ask your customer to be just as specific with you.

That's two points right there, player.

Rack up your third point with what the hell your customer is doing. Get the bigger context than just a sale. Get beyond the boundaries of your common business. What else is going on in your customer's career? Life? Dreams?

Three points. You are now free to move on.

But why stop? Keep racking up points. Even though there are no carryovers, meaning you can't carry the points from one scene into the next, it's still good practice. At that same breakfast with the customer, be clear about what the hell you're doing, too. What can you tell your customer that he or she doesn't already know about you? What will give her more clarity about you as a person?

By the end of the day, you will have cleared up a lot. Clarity is not a steady state, or a flat file. Clarity is dynamic. It requires constant questioning and refinement. And practice.

THE DAY YOU'RE DOWNSIZED

Your team is smaller today than it was yesterday. People who have been essential to your progress thus far are no longer on the journey with you.

It does not matter how this day comes about. It does not matter what prompted the downsizing. It does not matter if you survive the cut or if your services are no longer required. What matters is that you have fewer people supporting you and your work than you did before and just as much work to get done, if not more.

It is important to see this day as part of the normal landscape of the networked world. "Normal," you say? "What's normal about the bloat-and-shrink cycles many companies seem to follow, at the expense of their employees' loyalty and trust? What's normal about losing your job every six months or a year?"

Well, it's abnormal if you compare it to the past behaviors of Industrial Age companies, where repetition and machined growth were the status quo.

If you compare it to the way work gets done in the tech world, on a project basis, if you compare it to how artisans, small businesses and entertainers have spent all their professional lives, it's very normal. For entrepreneurs, it's standard procedure. Most don't know how they'll be earning an income from one year to the next. And yet they persevere, maintain and, quite often, thrive in this world of constant uncertainty. How do they do it?

Here's a game to experience this day in a whole new way and help you learn how lifetime contract workers create their success so you can apply their techniques on a day like today.

GAME OF THE DAY
SMALLER AND LARGER

Entrepreneurs are always weighing their odds, which change almost daily. The markets for their products and services are constantly changing and in those changes lie opportunities, because with each change, the odds of success change, too. Successful entrepreneurs maximize their bets on good opportunities and minimize their exposure when the odds are not in their favor. *Smaller and Larger* is a game that will train you to keep track of your odds of success as they *Shift* and, in the tracking, exert some *CTRL*.

At the beginning of the day, define a vision for your future. It might be a BHAG (Big Hairy Audacious Goal), or a MAUS (Minor Albeit Useful Scenario) that you believe is essential in some way to your eventual success. Now get a letter-sized sheet of paper (you can also do this with a mobile device) and write the word "Smaller" on one side and "Larger" on the other. Throughout the day, whenever you note anything that increases your odds of realizing your vision, list it on the "Larger" side of the paper. Whenever anything happens that lessens your odds of realizing your vision, list it on the "Smaller" side of the paper. These odds-shifting events can either be initiated by you or can happen outside your *CTRL*.

Halfway through the day, tally the lists to see if your odds of success have gotten Larger or Smaller. Note the patterns on each side of the paper. For the second half of the day, build on the patterns you've discerned on the Larger side of the paper. Do more of that. As much as possible, avoid the patterns and the people who create them you've noted on the Smaller side of the paper.

This is a formal way of practicing what comes naturally to entrepreneurs and to people who build long and productive careers as independent contractors. They are always nudging the odds in their favor. They realize that downsizing isn't as much about headcount as it is about missed opportunities. Even in a down market, you can learn to super-size your odds and opportunities.

DAY OF THE DEAD

Everywhere you look, you see zombies. People who are just going through the motions. People who feed on bad news. On the death of ideas and initiatives. They'll feed on you, too, if you're not careful.

Sometimes a little silliness is the best response to a Day of the Dead.

Surviving the day will depend on understanding and acting on the difference between the living and the dead. Basically, the difference is that the dead are incapable of being silly. Silliness is the test. If you are capable of being silly? Alive. Incapable of being silly? Dead.

Here is a dose of silly-making that can go far beyond the water cooler. Just make sure you establish the context for the game. You don't want your silliness to be mistaken for behavior detrimental to your team. You're lightening everyone's mood, not poisoning it. This isn't about attacking the zombies populating your day. This is about dancing with them, on the theory that maybe they'll start dancing, too.

GAME OF THE DAY
IF YOU KNOW WHAT I MEAN

Don't get sucked into negative energy. Keep things lively and fun. Animated vs. frozen.

To enliven things and bring the fun, you can play the *If You Know What I Mean* game.

Listen to the annoying conversations of people at work and add the phrase "if you know what I mean" to everything they say. Don't play it aloud. We don't want you to get fired. Just play it in your head. Then respond. It will help lighten up your day.

This is an example of what we call a 'silent yes-and.' The outcomes of this particular yes-and take the edge off edgy or intentionally incendiary comments, by turning them from emotional to meta language. If the office complainer complains about the air conditioning, or some other scenario you cannot do anything about, the game turns the complaint from incendiary to suggestive.

Like this:

The chronic complainer rants about the AC. Says, "It's too damn cold in here." Unless your role is building maintenance or keeper of the thermostat, there's not much you can do about it.

Ah, but if you have the game, the complaint becomes, "It's too damn cold in here (if you know what I mean.)"

Now we have ourselves a game. Something we can work with. Because when "cold" is a metaphor you can take it in a lot of different directions.

- "It's too damn cold in here." "Yes, I'm going to start smiling more."

- "It's too damn cold in here." "I know what you mean, let's have a party.'

- "It's too damn cold in here." "The coffee's still warm. Not hot. Warm."

- "It's too damn cold in here." "Yes, we should write the sequel to *Frozen*."

See what we mean?

You can play the game to create your own variations on the silent yes-end. Among the phrases we've silently tagged onto annoying or negative conversations, to our own amusement:

- "In Spain."

- "It's me, isn't it?"

And the always-dependable...

- "I read it in a book once."

INDEPENDENCE DAY

You have not done anything lately to distinguish your performance and, truth be told, you might be drafting on the energy of others to the point where you're dependent on it. On a day like today, you declare your intention to separate yourself from the field. The way you declare it is by doing it.

Whatever your routine has been, on a day like today, it's your nemesis.

Breaking away from the field does not always mean going faster. Your life is not the Tour de France or a Formula One track, with your fellow racers following the same route you are. Your path is unique to you. You're the only one living your life and doing your work the way you are. Besides, there is never only one way to get to your objective. A *Shift* in your direction or focus, even a slight one, can create a lot of separation between you and your co-dependents.

CTRL can give you your freedom. Structure can liberate performance. How you define and arrive at your independence is going to be up to you. Working faster is only one way of breaking away. In reality, you have an almost infinite variety of moves you can make on a day like today. All those moves are within your *CTRL*. And on the other side of that *CTRL...liberdade!*

Here's one move you can make on a day like today.

GAME OF THE DAY
TOUCHSTONE

As we said, your adversary on this day is your routine. Routines are circular. They repeat themselves. There's nothing wrong with this. We want and need aspects of our lives to be predictable, like paychecks and meals, just to name two. The issue with circular patterns is that there's no growth in sameness. The shapes of growth are spirals and rhizomes. Patterns that morph into new patterns. That's what you're going to play with today, with this game.

Here's how it works:

Draw a picture of your *Touchstone*, a certain thing you rely on, that comes predictably into play in your daily routine. Try to make it an object you use often. Maybe it's a stapler. Your coffee cup. A file folder. Your keyboard. A pen of which you are particularly fond.

Now, morph the drawing to become something else. What is it like if you turn the object upside down? What does an outline of it look like? What if you pulled both ends of it and stretched it as far as it can go?

Maybe...the coffee cup becomes a buffalo head. The stapler becomes ski jump. The file folder becomes a flat screen TV. The keyboard becomes an accordion. The pen becomes a telescope.

Let the experience of the game reflect onto your routine and your daily performance. Let it remind you that your routines are always adjacent to something unexpected and unique. Look at your life through a different lens and your experience of your life will transform. The same with a day like today. Just one slight *Shift* and everything can and will be different.

DAY OF SOLITUDE

On a day like today, you want to be alone. Solitude can be a precious gift, because it is so rare in a plugged-in world and so exceptional are the people who can embrace and appreciate it. What Lao Tzu said 26 centuries ago, when there was a lot more alone time available and it would not have been nearly as rare, "Ordinary men hate solitude. But the Master makes use of it, embracing his aloneness, realizing he is one with the whole universe."

If it was extraordinary 26 centuries ago for a person to choose solitude, think how exceptionally unusual it must be today. Already, by choosing this kind of day or letting it choose you, you are walking in rarified air. Congratulations, you're already ahead of the game.

Why do you want a day to yourself? Because you cannot get a clear picture of the universe, that thing a Master is one with, unless you quiet down and sit still. You can benefit from a day of solitude:

- after any extended period of exposure to humans or where you've spent significant time in a place where humans out-number other animals

- when you stink strangely of the road and you need to breathe in the friendly, familiar aromas of your homespace

- after you have done something that you are pretty sure won't turn out well for you and you don't need anyone to remind you of it

- when a stupid disagreement turns even stupider and you lock yourself in the bathroom, i.e. God's penalty box

Gather your gear and play the game, see you later.

GAME OF THE DAY
DO NOT DISTURB

This is a game to filter out noise of all kinds. Aural, visual, psychological—all of it combines to keep you from experiencing what the universe wants you to know about yourself and your relationship to your surroundings.

First, put up boundaries. Create a fortress for yourself. How you do this depends on your particular situation. Use whatever inventory you've got. Here are some ideas: give yourself an extra day on a business trip. Use those earbuds and construct a boundary of music, a soundtrack for your solitude. A long solo walk can describe a ˡ˄ry. So can police tape across the entrance to your

Next, rein in that social media. Estimate how many times in a day you check in on your social media channels. Cut it in half.

Do the same for email and phone calls. Estimate how many emails you send and respond to every day and halve those numbers. Those are your objectives for the day.

It would be rude not to attend your meetings. So attend your meetings. Don't say anything, though. Listen. If you have to speak, let it be to honor or help someone else in the meeting.

Cancel one meeting. Try not to be rude about it. Do it to a meeting whose scheduled attendees can benefit from the gift of having extra time in their day or conducting the meeting without you.

Establish one hour of complete silence. Unplugging. No texting. No emails. Nothing but solitude. If you know how to meditate, do it for an hour instead of the 15 minutes you usually schedule for it.

When you do find your solitude on a day like today, it will be important for you to quiet your mind. Who needs noisy solitude? What good is a hike through the wilderness with your mind screaming at you the entire time?

You can quiet your mind through a number of meditation and mindfulness techniques. You can do it by enlivening and paying attention to your body and your breath.

Celebrate your Day of Solitude by teaching people the Silent Cheer:

You: Give me a "Silent"

Them: SILENT!

You: Give me a "Cheer"

Them: CHEER!

You: Give me a "Silent Cheer"

Them: [raise fists in air and pump vigorously in silence]

Hat tip to a college classmate, Rick Esposto, for creating the Silent Cheer. It works with a small group and, if you want to make it truly stupendous, get several thousand people together like Rick used to and give it a shot.

THE DAY YOU QUIT

You thought this was going to be about quitting your job, didn't you? Well, that could be what it's about. But it could be about a whole lot more, too. It's the whole lot more we're interested in because today is "The Day You Quit" whatever it is you're doing that's become completely predictable, unsurprising and humdrum.

Start doing what will surprise people, yourself included. You are going to more-than-make-up for the unpredictability of your actions with the new possibilities you discover through them.

We never believed in the old cliché "Quitters never win and winners never quit." Winners quit all the time. They quit doing the things that get in the way of winning. Thomas Edison won the light bulb game when he quit burning through filament material in his lab experiments. To win the CEO job at Yahoo, Marissa Mayer had to quit Google. To win as Lady Gaga, Stefani Germanotta had to quit playing clubs in New York as Stefani Germanotta.

Winners *always* quit. In fact, it is a mark of winners that they are disciplined about what they quit, when and why.

Right now, you probably have a habit you oughtn't have. Just because you oughtn't have it, it doesn't mean it's a bad habit. We all get in the habit of repeating things we do well (and for good reason). For one thing, we get paid most predictably for what we do habitually well. For another, we need routine in our lives just so things don't get crazier than they already are.

The downside of the routine is that we're not growing. We're going in circles, doing laps around the same track. If the circle never morphs into a spiral, the scenery never changes and we never make a mistake, it's a sure sign we're not learning anything new. No one ever learned to walk without falling.

In improvisation, we call these predictable patterns in our behaviors our "go-to moves." In physics, they are called fractals or self-similar patterns. We must take pains to make sure we don't become overly-reliant on them. We must practice not repeating ourselves. We must assign ourselves scenes in which we are not allowed to use our go-to moves. Seek the inflection points that spin us out of circular patterns of fractals and into the spirals of future-shaping possibilities.

In improv comedy, a go-to move might be playing a character that always gets laughs.

In terms of work, a go-to-move might be that you always wait to be the last person in a group to speak. Maybe all your stories are about you. If you're in social media, maybe all your tweets are about your product. That's your go-to move. We have a client whose entire Twitter strategy consisted, prior to our intervention, of "Retweet." While we admire the simplicity of that, it's obvious that there's a lot more a brand can do in terms of its voice.

Go-to behaviors might work well for you, but they can also be a crutch. They can give you some solace, but they can also slow you down. In the long run, they're costly because they're limiting the possibilities you create for yourself.

Socially, a go-to-move can be anything from a dinner-and-a-movie date, to always beginning your romances in the gym, to calling your mom on Sundays. We know you got this. What else do you have?

"The Day You Quit" can be the day you acknowledge a go-to move in order to reduce your dependence on it. It can be "The Day You Quit" being so positive in order to be more reflective. It can be "The Day You Quit" talking so you can listen for a change.

Of course, there's also a chance that your go-to move is seriously bad for you. If you're coming to work straight from your workout, where you met your future wife, even though she doesn't yet know your name, without showering first...just quit, baby.

Here's a game to help you improve your quitting skills.

GAME OF THE DAY
THE GOOD, THE BAD AND THE UGLY

Quitting takes you into the unknown, because whatever you're doing, you're doing it without something you had when you were doing whatever it was you were doing before. It's an adventure! Because it's an adventure, it's not going to be a paved road. There are twists and turns. This game will help you deal with different aspects of the quitting process. We call these aspects *The Good, The Bad and The Ugly*.

Let's look at the act of quitting through these three lenses. As a thought experiment, you are going to play the scene that has you quitting whatever you're quitting in each of three ways. Then, you're going to eliminate the Bad, accentuate the Good and not mess with the Ugly.

Let's say, as a placeholder scene for the game, what you're quitting is the band. You're the lead vocalist and you're taking your pipes elsewhere.

Let's start with The Ugly. It's a very good place to start. Let's get this one out of your system. You walk into the garage where your band, "The Juice Boxxers," rehearse, and grab the microphone. You shout at the drummer that he has no rhythm and it's probably not the only place he has no rhythm. Then you turn to the guitar player and tell her she needs to take guitar lessons from someone other than her dad.

You unscrew and begin packing up your microphone that you paid for with your own money, but not before you brandish it like a magic wand that makes the bass player's meddling girlfriend go away.

And, oh yeah, just for good measure, you vomit on the sidewalk as you walk away. Your vomit spells out "Satan!" Too much? Yes, and that's exactly where you're at in your process. Ugly.

Now let's move on to Bad. You enter the garage and step up to the mic. The band members tell you that you are going to work on singing the cover song *Don't Stop Believing*. Just as you start to sing the second verse, you change the lyrics to:

"Just a stupid band

Playing in nowhere land

I took the express line train

To outta here."

You figured the best way to tell the band that you quit was to rewrite and sing the new break-up lyrics. The band members are disappointed. You have disparaged them musically, where it hurts. Color You Bad.

Now, let's go for the Good. You ask for five minutes of the band's time before your regular rehearsal. You begin by recounting the best experiences you've had with your bandmates, musically or otherwise. You thank them for these experiences. You tell them that you are looking to

Shift your priorities, now that you're turning 35 and have two kids and another on the way and you're going to have to give up your seat on Blaze, which is what you call the band's van. You have one last jam and part on good terms, after giving your bandmates several suggestions for lead singers who might be available for the Juice Boxxers' gig next weekend at the bowling alley bar.

Now, pick out what it is you want to quit and play this game. Once Ugly. Once Bad. Once Good. Then eliminate the Ugly, don't mess with the Bad and accentuate the Good for the rest of the day and forever after. Go!

THE DAY THE EARTH STANDS STILL

Everything comes to a full stop. No one moves. Nothing stirs. Animals quiet down. There's nary a breeze rustling nary a leaf.

In our frenetic world, a day like this one is rare and should be treasured as such. The stillness of the day is rich with opportunities that you probably would not notice if the day were spinning as madly as days usually spin.

Enjoy the stillness of a day like today and you might discover things like:

- Relationships you had not noticed before.
- Your voice.
- Your breath.
- Something that'll make you smile.
- Something that'll bring a tear to your eye.
- The details of your environment.
- A gift you've been given by someone who did not tell you they'd given it (probably because they did not know they'd given it).
- Patience.

On a day like today, you can't make things happen any more than you can stir a still forest, without setting it on fire, anyway. Otherwise, the environment resists all efforts to make it be anything but what it already is. Today, it's quiet in the woods.

One of the beautiful things about a Day the Earth Stands Still is that your discoveries are more within your *CTRL* than usual. Your *CTRL* is most complete when there's no perceptible *Shift* and that's the case today. What you discover on a day like today is going to be up to you. On a day like today, you are your own true north. There is no place to be other than where you are. No way to be, except as still as the day. Having grown still, you will see opportunities that you would miss if the day were a whirlwind.

Here's a game that will help you get the most out of a "Day the Earth Stands Still."

GAME OF THE DAY
A SLOW WALK TO NOWHERE

Find a place where you frequently walk the same path/ way each day. Pick a starting point of that path and walk in slow motion until the end of the path. On the way, try to see and hear things that you might have never noticed before. What sounds do you hear for the first time? What things do you discover? Use your senses to rediscover your path. At the end of your walk, sit in complete stillness for five minutes and observe the world around you with the senses you honed on your walk.

This game will help you improve your powers of observation on a day when lots of observing is possible. In stillness, you discover the subtle cues: the whispers and hints that you cannot see when everything's moving. The things you notice might be the solutions to a problem that's been nagging you or the missing piece to a puzzle you and your team have been trying to complete. Sometimes the answers are right in front of us, waiting to be noticed. All you have to do is take a slow walk to nowhere.

THE DAY YOU LOOSEN UP

The kind of day it is: you finally say "screw it, I've got nothing to lose," throw caution to the wind and fling yourself without reservation into whatever the day brings. You're loose, limber and elastic. You know why? You've stopped judging yourself and let yourself follow your instincts. Instinct, informed but not determined solely by intellect, is the optimal mode for decision-making. When you're loose, you're in that mode.

Back when the animation was hand-drawn, one of the highest compliments one Disney animator could give another was that his or her animation was "loose." This was huge praise. It meant that the lines and poses had a lot of life to them. They were drawn in the sweet spot between exaggeration and control. There was no "thinking" between the artist's hand and the paper, which would've tightened up the drawing, as the hand attempted to draw what the brain was imagining. Instead, the life of the artist literally flowed into the drawing. The liveliness of Disney artists who had rich lives outside animation—

they fly fished, flew planes, surfed, built trains, played music, performed magic, sculpted—all those experiences flowed from the hand to the paper unimpeded by the brain's need to meddle in such things. That's loose.

Now, in order to loosen up, let's be clear about what you don't want to think about. One has to be specific about these things. What you don't what to think about on a day like today is what its ultimate outcomes are going to be. To do what you're doing now and do it well, the last thing you want to worry about is what effect what you're doing now will have when you sum up the day later on.

Here's how you avoid thinking about outcomes: focus. You are focused on your objective. And just as important, you understand *why* you are doing what you do. There is a larger sense of purpose in play on a day like today. The tasks you have in front of you are graced by the larger purpose you serve. You can relax in that knowledge. It's not knowledge you have to use; it's knowledge that provides you with the space to stay loose. It's the foreknowledge that you have all the knowledge you need to accomplish what you're setting out to do, so you can maintain your focus on the task at hand.

We have friends with a non-profit company called *Spirit of Football*, who kick a soccer (foot)ball from the birthplace of modern soccer, in London, to the site of the FIFA World Cup every four years. They do it to raise money for schools and an education program called *One Ball, One World*. They make the trip on a shoestring budget, through 20-to-30 different countries. Everyone who crosses paths with the ball is invited to sign it. By the time it reaches its destination, it is the most-autographed ball in the world.

The Spirit of Football team is the definition of loose. They roll with whatever the day brings. In 2010, for example, on their way through Africa to the World Cup in Johannesburg, they had amazing adventures, almost all of them improvised. When they encountered setbacks, such as The Most Autographed Ball getting run over by a truck in the Ivory Coast, losing The Most Autographed Ball for three hours in Tanzania or having to cross the Namibian border without a visa, they adapted expertly in every situation.

(Namibian guards eventually autographed The Most Autographed Ball by stamping it with a visa, before letting the Spirit of Football team cross the border.)

What gave them the freedom to be this way? To travel with a loose idea of logistics and schedule, then play each day as it came and get the most out of it?

The Most Autographed Ball.

The Most Autographed Ball and, just as importantly, what it represents (fair play, unity, multiculturalism and our dreams of a better world) gave the *Spirit of Football* team its focus. In essence, they 'disappeared' into The Most Autographed Ball by becoming supporting players in a 6-month scene in which it was the star.

You can be loose today like the Spirit of Footballers, because you know what your Most Autographed Ball is, the thing you honor above all else. The thing that if everything but it were taken from you, you'd still be having a rich, full life. It's that thing you do and why you do it. You know what that is and you are going to have fun all day long, kicking it up the road and seeing whose path you cross along the way. People will see how important your Most Autographed Ball is and they will want to play along.

Here's a game the *Spirit of Football* team plays on their journeys. See how it works for you.

GAME OF THE DAY
100 REASONS

Write down 100 reasons why it's awesome to be around today. Doing it brain-dump style, so you surprise yourself.

Variation: Do it with a partner. Take turns listing 20 reasons at a time, until you both have 100.

Variation: Do it with a partner and list 20 reasons why it's awesome to have the other person around today.

Variation: Do it as a team and list 10 reasons per person why you appreciate people on your team.

THE DAY YOU FALL BEHIND

You've been so busy, you can't believe it's already ten o'clock! You haven't had a chance to look outside. You've been here since six AM, trying to get a jump on all these open tasks, and all you've been doing is falling farther behind. It could be storming outside and you would have no idea, because of the ****ing storm that's happening indoors.

Then the phone rings and it's your cousin who wants you to listen to what he did over the weekend and then your friend texts you to ask how the plans are coming along for her bridal shower. And then, and then, and then….

One unexpected thing after the next, after the next. The tasks you thought you would accomplish have not even been touched. So, if you weren't behind before, you are really behind now, with zero chance of catching up. What are you going to do?

You are going to improvise.

Treat your behind-ness with kindness. Play your way out of your deficit. Here's a game for that.

GAME OF THE DAY
KIND WALLS

"Be kind, for everyone you meet is fighting a hard battle," said Plato. And this is the theme of today's game.

As improvisers, we learn that the essence of productive action is focus. If you want your scene or your day to pay off, be fierce about maintaining your focus. In improvisation, the point of focus is a game. The game you play today has to be one that deals with your behind-ness. To do that, you'll need to eliminate or hold at bay anything and anyone who is not vital to your process and complete the tasks in front of you.

There are two ways of putting up these "walls" and being fierce about it. One that we've been guilty of (you probably have, too) is to snarl and bark at people like you're your own guard dog. A person innocently wanders into your space, you resent him instinctively, shoot him a look of death and send him away confused or offended. You answer a phone call that has nothing to do with your work and immediately put the caller on the defensive for reasons she cannot possibly understand. You'll be explaining your rudeness for a month.

The other way is to be kind but firm about your need for space.

So here's how to play it:

Play the cards that are already dealt and don't pick-up anything new. If you can do it without being rude, just say NO!

We know that sometimes you have to pick up new cards, so if that is the case, validate the person who needs your attention. Say "I hear you and I want you to know that I have a scheduled meeting or I have a deadline, so I will have to go in 5 minutes, let me know what's on your mind." Give that person your full attention in the moment and an understanding of what you have going on. Then everyone is on the same page. Time-box each interaction without coming across as rude, distracted or uninterested. Give people your full focus within strictly limited time frames.

Play this game and not only will you get more done by *CTRLing Shift*, if you're kind to people, you're bound to get kindness in return.

DRAFT DAY

On a day like today, you are guided by destiny's pull. Your name gets called. The light hits you. You discover just how much someone wants you. Your talent, charisma, character and leadership, along with a bit of good luck, figure into an organization's decision to make a significant bet on you. Your immediate future is staked to that bet. Congratulations! It feels good to be wanted, doesn't it?

Or does it?

Does getting drafted, in your case, feel like you're getting asked to raise the Titanic? Are you unprepared for the assignment? Is what you're being asked to do flat-out impossible? Do you feel as if you're a bad fit for your new team? Does what's described to you as a plum assignment feel more like a fruitless mission? Have you been drafted or have you gotten snagged in the ever-grinding gears of industry, a human lubricant in the big machine?

Either way, fasten your seatbelt, draftee, because you're getting tossed into the fierce flow of change. None of the old rules will apply. There will be new responsibilities associated with your new role. You'll be seen in a new light and will come under fresh scrutiny.

Oh, and there *will* be expectations. No matter whose expectations they are (yours, your boss's, your partner's or your dog's), there will be expectations. Understand one thing about them: your job is to kill them. Kill them before they get out of hand and unrealistic. It's not that you should set low expectations. That's no good either.

We're talking no expectations whatsoever.

Let yourself be completely open and free of the narrow restrictions your brain, even your right brain, fertile though it may be, places on you. You cannot imagine all the possibilities presented by a day like today, because you can only imagine what is already in your brain. When you are open and without expectation of judgment, you are fueling your imagination when it can help you most and expand possibilities the most—*in the moment!*

How do you kill expectations? By getting away from self-judgment and the constant scripting your brain does about what might happen, in order to keep you and your team focused in the Now. With the focus and presence made possible by your game, you are oblivious to the weight of history or the airiness of an uncertain future. You can be fully present to the possibilities that your new assignment offers you on a day like today.

Here's your ticket away from the friendly confines of your brain, into the wide open space of the Now.

GAME OF THE DAY
NO BRAINER

This game comes to us from our friend, Dr. Debra Hockenberry, who was the first woman in the U.S. to play Division I college soccer, when she competed for the NYU Men's soccer team in the late 1960s. Today, she is an 'organizational ninja,' who teaches business transformation techniques at universities throughout the eastern U.S. Let's just say Debra's got game.

Because expectations live in our head, killing expectations on a day like today means taking our heads out of the equation completely and learning to trust our bodies, our senses and our instincts in unbridled intra-action with the world. This game, according to Dr. Hockenberry, who has a particular interest in alchemical studies, was practiced by the Alchemists of the Middle Ages, as a precursor to their day's work.

The Alchemists knew that learning about the world and describing what they learned came from a fully embodied experience and could not be solely accounted for by the working of the mind.

To perform this exercise, you will need a mirror, a pen, a blank piece of paper and a piece of paper with a semi-intricate pattern, such as a mandala or a maze, printed on it. (See Photo.)

Sit at a table or desk with a partner. (It is also possible, with a little arranging of the materials, to do this exercise solo.)

Place the paper with the pattern on the table in front of you, pattern-side up. Your partner (or you) holds the blank piece of paper between you and the pattern so that you cannot see it or your writing hand. (See Photo).

Your partner then holds the mirror at an angle, so you can see your writing hand and the paper with the pattern. You will, of course, see it in reverse.

While watching your writing hand in the mirror, practice tracing the pattern. Begin with the outermost line.

It is very likely that you will find this difficult. This is because you cannot use your brain to guide your writing

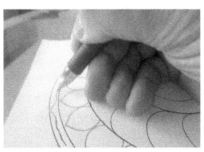

hand. It is completely counter-intuitive. You have to feel your way as you trace your pattern. In other words, only your sense of touch and movement, your material intra-action with pen, paper and sight, can show the way. Your thinking brain is no good to you here. Sense the line you're drawing. Don't try to think the line into existence. Feel it.

Please give Dr. Debra Hockenberry thanks and credit when you play this game or share it. Her email address is pearlbh@aol.com.

THE DAY YOU SAY GOODBYE

The kind of day it is: you have known for some time that this day is coming. You never really gave much thought to how you'd approach it and, now, here it is. It finally hits you.

You're going to say goodbye.

You don't really like goodbyes and would rather slink away unnoticed, but these people, in this world you're leaving behind, have figured into your life. The relationships you've developed, to be tested by distance and time, mean something and you'd fall short on the basic level of being human if you didn't acknowledge their meaning.

The *Shift* on a day like today has you moving away from an environment that has shaped your life so that other environments can, in their own ways, affect your life, too. If you never say goodbye, if the environment that sustains you never changes, you get to be like a zoo animal, whose behaviors never change and who may even turn neurotic and unnatural.

Zoo animals don't have a choice. You, you sexy beast, have a choice and you're making it. You're going somewhere. First, though, there's this goodbye thing to deal with.

Remember that when you say goodbye, you become a symbol to those you're leaving behind. Begin your goodbye by letting go of our own sentiments. Park them until you've driven away and bawl your eyes out on the road. Put some structure and discipline to the day to help you make the most of it and, more importantly, make the most of it for those you're goodbyeing.

Be the symbol. Represent the adventuring, the bold choices and the self-reliance that you are going to symbolize after you say goodbye. Leave the mushiness of your goodbye to those you're leaving behind. Be solid and memorable, not mucked up in the swale of your premature nostalgia. This game will help you structure the day and make sense of it, so that you walk away with everyone feeling good about what's next, for you and those to whom you say goodbye.

GAME OF THE DAY
SOUNDTRACK

Music accompanies us everywhere, sets a tone, evokes memories, inspires us and helps us escape. You're going to hack this day by continually reminding yourself of this wonderful reality. You're going to do it by composing a very special, one-of-a-kind *Soundtrack* for the Day, made up of song titles that suit every scenario you find yourself in.

Here's how it works, as an example.

The day begins with nagging kids. They are on your case before you wake up. One of them has the sniffles and is in a cranky mood, which puts you in a cranky mood, too. Another is so bright and chipper and rosy that it only reminds you of how cranky you are. Clearly, this is the Johnny Cash rendition of *Folsom Prison Blues,* and then, before you have a mental breakdown *La Vie Boheme.*

Having turned heartache into art, you're waltzing into your car and off to work. You get cut off off in traffic by a clueless driver talking on the phone and looking at himself in the rear view mirror at the same time. The first finger-snapping notes of the Jets and the Sharks in *West Side Story's, Jet Song* echo in your head. Or maybe a Lil Wayne song? The rest of your commute is a roving turf war. Pay attention or there'll be a price to pay.

You get the idea. Accompany your day with music. Don't use it as an escape from the mundane; use it to transform the mundane by adding music. It will help you contextualize your actions and elevate the everyday into the extraordinary.

Have you ever seen an action film or a romance without a music *Soundtrack?* It hardly feels like action or romance at all.

Put the action and the romance into your day. What is your soundtrack for the day? Move to it. Groove to it. Have yourself a Day.

MOVING DAY

Everything is in boxes, packaged and labeled. Now, all you have to do is kick back, sip a cup of coffee and wait for the movers to arrive. You'll then check into a hotel for the night, at your company's expense, before a leisurely drive to your new location, a drive that'll include stops at two national parks, a hot springs spa and two restaurants featured on The Food Network.

You wish.

That's "Dream Moving Day," the kind of day that only happens for people in TV commercials. It's like winning the Powerball Lottery that way. The odds are that the way this day gets advertised is not how it's going to be for you.

Here's the real *"Moving Day"*: madness! You awaken in a pre-dawn panic and it only gets worse from there. No matter what time the movers arrive, you will not be ready. What began as a process of neat labeling and smooth taping of boxes dissolves into you dumping whole drawers of stuff into unlabeled boxes secured with tape that you've had to bite off the dispenser like a rabid animal chewing its way out of a snare.

The emptiness of the old space works on you until you feel empty, too. You are not, on a day like today, moving toward your new destination as much as you are creating a limbo of neither here nor there, a *Shiftless* place between the hell of moving and the heavenly promise of a fresh start. Your job is to get this *Shift* on the road. Gear up. Get going. Refocus.

We have a game for that.

GAME OF THE DAY
SIGN STORIES

This game will work for you whether you're on the road or still packing. Whatever stage of moving you're at, you can play it to add *CTRL* to your imminent *Shift*.

During your day, you'll see names of places you've never been before, for example, on signs that indicate origins or directions. Every time you see the name of a place you've never been before, tell yourself a story about it. What kinds of people live there. What the main industry might be. Make up a name for the mayor of the place. Give a team nickname to a high school there. Describe its most prominent geographical and architectural features.

This game is a design for a meditation on moving. As you go through the more mechanical processes of the move (changing of addresses, handoffs of keys, sealing of records, labeling of boxes, etc. etc. etc.), it will have two types of outcomes that will ease your day: 1) it will remind you not to script the experiences that await you and not to prejudge anything or anyone about it; 2) it will remind you that we are all responsible for the way we see and respond to change.

By *CTRLing* your response and your perspective on your new environment, you can turn your particular *Shift* into anything you want it to be. Not today. But soon. When the time comes, you will be ready, because you are the teller of your own story.

THE DAY OF YOUR IPO

In terms of your professional life, this is one of the most *Shift*-filled days there is. This is the day the river card gets dealt in a high-stakes game with your organization all-in. Everything is about to change. No matter how the cards come up, lots of money is going to change hands today.

Money? Money changes everything. Maybe it shouldn't, but it does. By the end of the day, the investment your organization has made could pay off big-time and you can all begin planning your fairy tale weddings in Sherwood Forest.

Dreams? Today's the day you find out if dreams come true. Will it be a future you imagined? Or one that surprises you?

No matter what happens, don't expect a carefree skip through the park. Being careless did not get you where you are today and it won't be what characterizes your future. No, on a day like today, you're going to be trading one set of problems for another.

Maybe the new problems will be more fun to solve. The waiting list for a Tesla is *how long?* Why is Anthony Bourdain not returning your calls about *opening a restaurant together?* Maybe not. Your accountability to your investors will be a far cry from your rollicking garage start-up phase, when you were accountable to your wealthy aunt, your landlord and your dog.

George Lucas used to tell his screenwriters, "Begin the new story with the end of the previous story." The end of one story is always the beginning of another. When today begins, your old story ends. Welcome to the new day. Congratulations on all your hard work. Here's a gift.

GAME OF THE DAY
RIPPED FROM THE HEADLINES

Imagine the headlines exactly a year from now. What will the headlines say about you and your company? Write fake articles for the headlines. See what major points come out of it. Add visuals to the newspaper. Why would your followers repost to their networks? Are their motivations and intentions aligned with your strategic goals for the coming year?

Post this article where you can see it everyday to remind you where you are going and where you want to be.

You can take this as far as mocking up a series of headlines and stories for one year from now. They don't just have to be about your company. What else will be going on in the world at that time? Who will be making money and who will be losing money? What events will transpire in the worlds of sports, politics and entertainment? Have some fun by hazarding guesses.

If you want to take it even farther, you can make a kind of time capsule, to be opened in a year, or designate a bulletin board for *Stories from the Future* and encourage your team to aggregate all kinds of predictions there.

You get the idea. Call some shots, however you want to do it. And then work at making them come true.

THE DAY YOU DO WHAT SCARES YOU

It's the day you quit talking about it, obsessing about it, shying away from it, speculating about it...and do it.

Get out your parachute. Learn to skydive before you jump. But for God's sake, jump!

Jump with the confidence that when you do, you'll fly.

Research shows that public speaking terrifies more people in business than anything else. Let's say for the past year you have had your sights set on a national conference. You really would love to be a speaker, if it didn't involve you having to speak in front of people. You would rather die than give a talk, but you know in order to build your personal brand, you have to put yourself out there in the limelight and be seen as an expert in your field.

To build up the courage to speak on this stage, think of topics and work on a talk. Practice giving the talk to a group of co-workers and not just to your bathroom mirror. Then face your fear, jump onto stage and own it. You'll land before you know it.

You can do this with whatever scares you. The saying in improv theater coined by the legendary Del Close is "Follow the fear." What Del meant by that is if you're doing something that scares you, you're expanding your horizons and your talent. You are doing the scariest thing of all—exploring the unknown. This is the area of real growth. It is the liminal space where babies learn to walk and champion athletes set world records by pushing beyond their known limits. When you follow the fear, you experience the potential you cannot realize when you let your fear stand in the way.

GAME OF THE DAY
MICHAEL BAYWATCH

This game is named for a well-known faux-pas at the 2014 CES convention when the film director, Michael (*Transformers*) Bay, lost his way during a presentation for Samsung when his teleprompter malfunctioned. Without the teleprompter script, Bay was so helpless and lost, he had to leave the stage.

This game will help reduce your and your team's need for a crutch and help make you more independent and self-reliant. It will help you realize that your intelligence can contribute to any scene, as long as you let it, and are willing to let go of the script that has been written for you or the structure dictated by the status quo. It will prepare you for the inevitable day when the teleprompter goes haywire, so that you don't. It goes like this:

Work with a partner or a group of people. Pick a book off a bookshelf that has relevance to your work or life skills. Read (or have someone read) aloud from it. When someone says "Michael Bay," close the book and, as seamlessly as possible, keep going with your own version of whatever you were reading.

This is great practice for creating self reliance, for calling on your reserves of intelligence and presence that are not required when you're relying on a script. When all you've got is your script, you're vulnerable, because losing your script is the equivalent of losing all your power to perform.

Having a script or a teleprompter is fine. There's nothing wrong with compiling and documenting your best thoughts, your most inspiring ideas. What's wrong is the belief that your best thoughts and most inspiring ideas belong to the script and not to you, and when the script goes away, so must you. This game will let you kick the crutches out of that crippling mindset and give you the moves to perform on your own, no matter what your environment or your scene partners throw your way.

GAME DAY

There's a big event today with a lot riding on it. Your and your team's professional standing, your contract, your media content, ticket sales, customer loyalty, customer influence and most aspects of your business are going to be affected by your performance on a day like today.

Own it! Get your game face on. Prove you're a player, that you belong in the big leagues. This game will help.

GAME OF THE DAY
PLAY IT LIKE A PRO

Nowhere is the concept of game more important than in the lives of professional athletes. If there was ever proof that games generate many outcomes (and that the game's objectives and its outcomes are different), it's the pro athlete's relationship with his or her game. Income, opportunities, relationships, name recognition, fan loyalty, these are just a few types of outcomes the pros realize as a result of playing their games.

When the stakes are high and you've got to get your game on, take a professional athlete's approach to your performance. Play it like a pro. Here's how:

Choose 3 to 5 of these elements of performance. Work through them with focus and attention to detail in order to perform at a high level on a day like today. Endorsement deals and gear with your name on it are sure to follow.

1. X's and O's.

Diagram every scenario you expect to encounter during the day. Who will be on the field, in the arena, on the grid with you? What moves will people make? What kind of defenses do you expect to encounter? Find a whiteboard and channel your favorite coach, talking to your favorite team. Diagram each play on a separate sheet of paper. When you're done, put these sheets in a binder. This is your playbook.

2. Scouting and Walk Through

Get a sense of the field of play and the tendencies of the other players. If you're on a team, conduct a quick, very loose rehearsal and warm-up.

3. Pep Talk

This can be in-person or online. You can give it to yourself, your team or both. Use it to get at your and your team's motivation, your sense of purpose. Define what it is you have to prove. Name the little boy in the hospital bed or the family who needs you to win this one for them. Who is your personal Gipper? Look at YouTube videos of coaches giving great speeches for your inspiration. What is your equivalent? What unites your team? What will a winning performance look and feel like on a day like today? All of this can be brought front and center and put into focus by a rousing pep talk.

4. Your Fight Song

It can't be *Eye of the Tiger*, you're better than that.

5. CTRL Tempo

Think about the speed at which you will go through today. Figure out when to speed it up or when to slow it down. Think and act like a point guard, a catcher, a midfielder, a silly mid-off (that's cricket, son). If things are moving too quickly (never really a problem in cricket) and threaten to get out of hand, slow it down. Make sure everyone checks in, that you can see one another. If the tempo feels sluggish, speed it up.

Sometimes changing the tempo of a day for no other reason but to change it can produce beneficial outcomes. Simply by making yourself and those around you more aware of the tempo and timing of things, you become more aware of one another and more supportive as a result. *CTRLing* tempo is a good way to find your flow.

6. Make Halftime Adjustments

Okay, you're at the midway point of your day. You know what this means: halftime entertainment. This happens while you, as a player, make your halftime adjustments.

What did you learn in the first half that will benefit you in the second half? How will you adapt to game conditions? How will you account for the way others are playing? Good players always heighten their performance in the second half.

7. Gut Check

The bold and adventurous will soar on a day like today.

If we turn away from our fear and only do what's safe (i.e. take a path we've taken before), we never grow, never realize the possibilities we have for expressing ourselves. We can't see the possibilities, because we let our fear get between us and them. We turn away.

**** that! On a day like today, turn into your fear. Do something that scares you. You'll discover a part of yourself you never would've known if you'd let your fear get in your way.

8. Shake Hands With Yourself

Treat the *Game of the Day* not as something you have to do, but as something you get to do.

Will you react with your logical self or emotional self? List the day's events and challenges and then play through each of them, once with your logical self, once with your emotional self. Decide whether logic or emotion will be more effective. Whichever you decide, give yourself that aspect of *CTRL* if and when you encounter each scenario.

THE DAY THE COMPETITION MAKES A MOVE

The kind of day it is: You and your team get caught off-guard when your competitor makes a move you don't expect.

You pride yourself on your market intel. You like to feel you know what's going on out there: what your customers are thinking, where demand will be in six months, how your brand differentiates itself and how it offers unmatched value. You are confident in where your story is going.

Your competitors for your customers' attention have stories, too. On a day like today, your story takes an unexpected twist because theirs does. And suddenly you feel the audience's attention *Shift* to (shudder) *them*.

What's a player to do?

Have we got a game for you! Check it:

GAME OF THE DAY
SHOT CALLER

A *Shot Caller* is a street slang term that means someone of high status in a gang, one who gives orders and establishes the game. A shot caller has street smarts and prefers common sense tactics to the predictable formulas of a business school education.

The Urban Dictionary [http://www.urbandictionary.com] has 10 definitions of "shot caller." Here they are, listed in order of upvotes by the site's users:

1. *An individual in a gang who has a high status. This person "calls the shots," but he doesn't carry it out, he's already done that role, hence his elevated status.*

2. *Someone who calls the shots*

3. *An individual who runs the prison, even respected by the guards. The warden of the inmates, runs the asylum, unbreakable, high commissary status, most likely a lifer and deadly, always keeping people from taking his place.*

4. *The person responsible for calling out the final "payoff" shot on a porn shoot.* [These came from the internet; what did you think would get votes?]

5. *A baller; a player; someone who calls all the shots around him.*

6. *He/she who calls the shots. i.e. decides what's going down.*

7. [Our favorite] *One who sees all and allows others to control the aim until the shot caller feels the need to guide.*

8. *One who purchases "called shots" (IE those that are more expensive such as Hennessy or Grey Goose) rather than cheaper "well" drinks.*

9. *A baller who exhibits cockiness and attitude by yelling "in," "nothin' bu' net," "money" etc. before his shot hits the rim, in an effort to imply that he is skilled enough to place full confidence upon his shot without seeing the result.*

10. *A word used in* [the video game] *Counterstrike; Someone that walks into a warzone and leaves it while alive.*

Today, you're going to create the 11th definition of "shot caller." This definition will be the code you live by, your *omerta*, for today.

You need a crew; who will be in it? What roles do you want them to play? You're the shot caller; you decide. You need an executive sponsor, a teacher or a mentor. Who will it be? What are the qualities you want in a teacher? What do you need to learn? Make a list. Do this for all the players you want rampaging with you today.

You need a sidekick. Who will it be? List the qualities you envision in a sidekick. It should be someone whose abilities and temperament complement yours.

No words or few words are necessary to be a Shot Caller. Make your words count. Give them weight. Use pauses for dramatic effect. Call the shot. Then make the shot. It's as simple as that. With practice, more and more of your called shots will be good.

FAN APPRECIATION DAY

On a day like today, you create raving fans for what you do. Every idea you have is a home run or a touchdown or a knockout or a checkmate or a standing ovation or a pile driver of a body slam for the win.

People want a piece of you. A slice of your pie. They want to frost your cake. Butter your biscuits. People want to drink from your fountain. Not only do they drink your water, they will carry your water for you. And wipe up your dribbles.

People want their picture taken with you. They want to buy you gifts.

Yes, as you and the Rolling Stones both know, it's good to have fans.

When you and all you do are appreciated in such ways by your fans, there's only one thing you can do for your fans. Appreciate them back.

Here's a game for that.

GAME OF THE DAY
FAN CLUB

As the star of your day, you are going to model the behavior of celebrities who have healthy, collaborative relationships with their fans. Here are suggestions for the kinds of behaviors that would be consistent with your role as Star Who Appreciates Fans:

Sign lots of stuff. Anything that requires your signature, sign it. Fill out applications. Pay bills. Send notes. Nobody does that anymore, except you, because you appreciate your fans. Do it with a flourish. Add some pizzazz to your autograph. Your fans expect that.

Take photos of yourself with your fans. Every photo you take today must be of you and at least one of your fans. No landscapes or selfies. Today, it's all about the fans. If you use your own device to take a photo, you must send the fans in the photo with you a copy of the photo before the end of the day. Because that's how you treat a fan club right.

Post an album on Facebook of pictures of you with your fans.

Post up in your *green room*, your space where you can prepare before you take the stage. All stars have a place adjacent to their stage where they can rest, focus and get away from the hullabaloo and foofaraw of the fans for a minute. You need your space, too. It could be a restroom or a break room or your car or the steps by the back door.

Make a fan appreciation video and post it on YouTube. Curate a YouTube album of other stars, like Elvis, Michael, Leonardo, Aretha and Bieber thanking their fans.

Dress to be seen. It's not so much that you're self-conscious, more that you're self-aware when you're playing the *Fan Club* game.

Reward your fans by playing off their expectations of you. What are some of your signature moves? Make them. Your fans expect them as surely as they expected a moonwalk from Michael Jackson or count on seeing Bjork in an ingenious wardrobe.

Make an appearance and put on a show. At some point, your fans expect you to deliver what made them fans in the first place. Do it. What is your stage? Your zone? Own it. Claim your fame.

We don't normally advocate this, but a *Fan Appreciation Day* doesn't come around that often: if you see wet concrete at any time during the day, go ahead and sign your name in it, the way the stars do at the Chinese Theatre in Hollywood. This will give your fans fond memories of you whenever they see it. That's your obligation. That's how you roll as a star. You do it for the fans.

SEVERE TURBULENCE DAY

The kind of day it is: all hell is breaking loose! What are you doing even reading this? There's no time, because all hell is breaking loose! One minute, things were fine. And now this?! What the--?! This isn't supposed to be happening. This is not what you bargained for. You thought you had everything under control and now...

ALL HELL IS BREAKING LOOSE!!!

What are you waiting for? All hell is breaking loose! Get to gaming!

GAME OF THE DAY
HAPPY AND GRUMPY

This game takes ten minutes to play and it will more than pay you back in the course of a ****ing day like today.

You will need a partner. The two of you will take turns telling a story about a subject that can be either real and practical, such as a work scenario (e.g. a turf war between two managers) or imagined and whimsical (e.g. a story about a magic raincoat or Mary's Little Lamb).

One of you (Happy) says good and positive things to begin the story, such as, "Once upon a time Mary had a beautiful little lamb. Its name was Aphrodite. It followed her to school one day."

The other storyteller (Grumpy) tells the next part of the story and it's all negative, as in, "Aphrodite had a bad case of fleas and Mary was itching that day, too. The lamb also had a bad case of hoof rot."

Then the Happy storyteller follows, "Mary was able to turn her itching into a new dance step. The children made a video of her dancing at recess that went viral."

If you're feeling animated, you can mime the story as you tell it, do Mary's dance. You can do it for an audience and take turns sharing your stories in a small group (of no more than eight people, four pairs of storytellers).

When you have told the story for five minutes, end it happily, tragically or however ambiguously you want it to conclude. Make a list of all the things the Happy storyteller said in telling the story. Sum up the Happy point of view. How does that person see the world? Do the same for the Grumpy person.

Now rip up the Grumpy list and throw it away. It's useless to you and everyone around you. Make two sets of the Happy list and point of view. You and your partner carry those around all day and use them as your lens on the world. Using the Happy point of view will help keep hell where it belongs, separate and apart from you, as all of it breaks loose on a ***ing day like today.

A FUNNY DAY

You know early on it's going to be one of those funny days. Slapstick in the bathroom is an early indicator. A child's room that is so pathetically beyond cleaning up before school that all you can do is laugh with each other. Or that child mumbling half asleep nonsense. Nothing says "Day That's Going to Turn Comical" like a drink spit take at breakfast. So, be on the lookout.

It'll only get funnier at work. Random whiteboard cartoons, self-deprecating bosses, something unidentifiable in the break room fridge, these are all solid on the guffawmograph, as are co-workers with stories of disastrous dates the night before and that meme everyone is sharing today. On a day like today, everything is just plain lulzy.

Humor is a wonderful way to release tension and bond. It is the happiest way we've got of learning from our mistakes.

There's two kinds of yuck. Today's is the good kind. Enjoy it!

GAME OF THE DAY
COMIC STRIP

Pick two or three people you work with and create your own comic strip about something comical that happened to you at work. Exaggerate words, poses, traits and situations from real life to make them fit into a comic strip genre.

Variation: Photocopy a favorite comic strip with the captions and speech balloons whited out and have a contest in the office to see who can fill them in and come up with the best comic strip about the office. Have a showing at the end of the day.

Second variation: You can repeat this every day for a week, with a different comic strip, and have the showing at the end of the week.

Note: this game should only be played with people who know one another, have built up trust and acceptance and are willing to laugh at themselves and their foibles. This game is not for the easily-slighted, the new employee who hasn't established himself in terms of being a known personality or the boss who's an excessive needler. In that case, just circulate a couple of classic *Calvin and Hobbes* comics and call it a game.

THE DAY YOU GET TOO BIG

Too many people CC'ed on emails. Too many people in meetings. Too many sign-offs required on what should be a simple decision. You know more of your co-workers on LinkedIn than you do in person.

Two security badges required on official company lanyard. Fines for missing lanyards get assessed via facial recognition software licensed from Homeland Security.

Break room gets replaced with a Panda Express.

Company softball team now composed completely of players from the Dominican Republic who'd once been in the Dodgers' farm system.

Company sexual harassment video produced by Pixar.

You're too big. Time to slim it down, shed weight and get more nimble. Here's a way:

GAME OF THE DAY
GET SMALL

If your life were a musical score (and who's to say it isn't?), this is the day you go all *pianissimo* on its ass.

In lay terms, you get quiet. Soft. Gentle. The bigness of your organization is not your jam. Nor is it within your *CTRL*. Sometimes, *Shift* itself is a form of *CTRL*. Today, you shift into a quiet gear. You glide instead of stomp. Whisper instead of scream.

The *Get Small* game requires focus on your voice, your movement, gestures and sensitivity to your environment, because that's what getting small is all about. It's about shrinking the space you and your team are taking up, diminishing the bandwidth you're using.

There are three guidelines to the game:

Lower your normal speaking volume. This will make communication more intimate and give it more gravitas. It will get people leaning in. It will improve listening and help order chaotic communication environment. And when you do decide to underscore an idea, you will be doing it that much more forcefully, just by speaking at your normal volume.

Consolidate communication. Clean up your email. Eliminate unnecessary CC'ing. Hold fewer and faster meetings. Delegate more, so that communication can be more direct and involve fewer back-and-forths between managers.

Let someone go. Now, there is a harsh way of doing this and that, of course, has to do with downsizing. Firing someone. It happens, it is inevitable under certain conditions and it almost always sucks. Ideally, in letting someone out of their current situation, you'll be pointing them toward a better path than the one they're on now.

This guideline is not really about that, though. It's about realizing that there are many ways to "let someone go" and acting on that notion. For instance, it can be about manners. Let someone go ahead of you. It can be about knowing an employee's child has a dance recital and letting that person go early to attend. It can be about relieving someone of a responsibility for which they have no authority, thus freeing her to be more accountable and engaged in the mission. Also, this helps eliminate any role redundancy. No one on a team benefits from that, especially the players whose roles overlap.

With the *Get Small* game, you address the biggest weaknesses of bigness. You get quicker, better able to maneuver and be in position to help get to your objectives. Your appetite shrinks, so you can get more done with less fuel. You become more sensitive to your surroundings. When your game gets too big, your bigness slows you down. When you downsize your game and simplify your process, you'll get faster instead of fatter.

THE DAY YOU LAUNCH

Well, well, well, here we are.

After all the work, all that coding, testing and customer interviewing, and testing, and budgeting and architecting, and testing and testing and testing and testing, and debugging and testing some more, we have arrived at the day we go live, just as soon as we finish testing.

You know it's going to just get crazier, because no launch in the history of launches gets through clean. There will be bugs. Glitches. Issues. It's the nature of the beast.

How do you control the beast that lurks just beyond the launch? A beast that can rip you limb from limb and destroy you if it gets loose?

You play. And you play as a person whose life does not hinge on a day, but rather on the long arc of vision and narrative, a vision that is persistent and strong and a narrative that, while it takes twists and turns, always rewards. For every setback, there is a helper. For every twist, a delightful surprise.

GAME OF THE DAY
LEGION OF SUPERHACKERS

This game is inspired by every superhero comic and movie ever. *"The Day You Launch"* is the kind of day when it's important to summon your Superhacker powers. Yours and every member of your team's. No Superhacker stands alone.

You are about to enter an extraordinary world, unlike the world you are leaving behind, and you're going to need more than your everyday superpower of being able to find a parking space.

Your *Legion of Superhackers* equates to your Fantastic Four, your X-Men, your Power Rangers.

Your objective is to accumulate Superhacker points by accomplishing various tasks and, at the same time, vanquish the monsters that stand between you and a successful launch.

Begin by naming the Legion members. Which Superhacker will you be? Who will be your fellow Superhackers and what will their names and powers be? Here are some suggestions. As always, feel free to hack your own names, powers and game guidelines:

Flame is raw and direct, confronts situations intuitively, heightens emotions.

Denim takes the long view, shows patience, persistence, honors history and legacy.

Sapphire possesses superb analytical skills, sees patterns that others cannot.

Lime enlivens everyone and everything, gets attention, adds superhuman value.

Quartz is the curious experimenter, champion of the scientific method.

Amber makes connections and mashes ideas together. Always asks "What if?"

A key aspect of the game is that, while you have Superhacker powers in a particular area of performance, you are at your best when you are working with a Superhacker with a different superpower. If you're Denim, team up with Flame to cover the full emotional spectrum, from patience to passion. If you're Lime, you can team with Quartz to make your scientifically sound experiments more fun and engaging and get the most out of the experimentation by adding zest and flavor to it.

Next, compile a list of five tasks you want to get done or managed today. These cannot be ordinary, run-of-the-mill tasks. They must be tasks that challenge the Superhacker in you. So give them extraordinary names.

"Add Help Desk Support" becomes "Reinforce Dinoblaster Shield"

"Offer Free Downloads to Influencers" becomes "Seers Receive Gifts from Gods"

"Key Account Guidance" turns into "Swear Allegiance to the Five Thrones"

"Email Blast" morphs into "Release the Crows!"

Assign each task a Damage Rank from 1 to 5, with 5's being tasks that will do the most damage if they're not completed, 1's the least. Work fast; the planet depends on it!

Next, assign each task a Reward Rank from 1 to 5, with 5's being tasks that will reward you most if they're completed, 1's the least. Go, go, go!

Add the Damage and Reward Rankings. Highest numbers have the most ability to affect you on a day like today.

Next, identify 3 Dread Monsters you'll inevitably confront during the day. As before, the names of the ordinary world morph into names befitting a challenge to a superhero such as yourself.

"Call Center Glitches" might translate to "Evil Phone Spells"

"Can't Reach the Owner for Key Decision" becomes "Stolen Cloak of Invisibility"

"Content not getting passed through mobile app" turns into "Constipated Dragon"

Work in teams of four, with each member of the team taking on a different Superhacker power.

Every time you team up with a fellow Superhacker hero to complete a Heroic Task, each of you score the number of points you have ascribed to that task.

And every time you team up with a fellow Superhacker to confront a Dread Monster, each of you scores the points awarded for bringing

Etc. etc. etc.

Ultimately, how you score it is up to you. What, you didn't expect us to figure out the whole game for you, did you? What fun would that be? Figure it out for yourself. Make the game your own.

Total the scores at the end of the day. Let yourself be surprised by who is the top Superhacker. Make it more about the story of the day than about the score. Everyone treats the top Superhacker to something yummy.

Good luck, Superhackers! Power up! Join forces! Overcome the monsters that seek to destroy you! Collect bonus points and add Superhacker powers! Hack on!

GROUNDHOG DAY

Named in honor of the classic Bill Murray film, it is as if everything is repeating today is repeating is repeating is repeating. Deja vu awaits at every turn. There's a sameness to the day that makes you feel like a hamster on a wheel.

On a day like today, people are too predictable to be stimulating. Decisions don't get made; they get prolonged. The only decisions actually made are the firm and unwavering commitments by your co-workers to never decide on anything. Your world is a thousand channels of reruns and movies you've seen before.

The challenge of a day like today is that you feel as stale as a week-old loaf of bread. Since you know what people are going to say before they say it, the invitation is to always respond the same way yourself, to be as predictable as your scene partners.

Since no decisions are getting made, you become indecisive yourself, just to play along. You let the inertia of the *Groundhog Day* drag you along.

Well, guess what? *Groundhog Day* is a great big illusion. It's your perception. Things are not the same, day in and day out. Do you know what's different about today? Your response to it. Do you know who's not predictable, who's capable of surprising everyone with a performance that has not been scripted, memorized and repeated until even the audience knows it by heart? You are.

Here's how to play it.

GAME OF THE DAY
UP A NOTCH

Oh, the monotony of routine!

Today, let's change things up to see how you can affect the outcome of your own personal *Groundhog Day* movie. Look around you, consider your options for a minute and find something you use, do, or say repetitively everyday. Maybe you always sit in the same spot at the morning meeting. Or use the same color whiteboard marker. Or speak to the same people in the course of a day. What can you change to break your repetitive cycles?

It can be a simple change of shifting your chair up a notch. It could be changing the over-used phrase "At the end of the day" to "At the end of the picnic." Or "At the end of the parade." It could be quieting yourself and speaking to your boss without blinking, when normally you're a bag of tics, blinks and squirminess. See what that does to your day. How does it change your perspective? Your response to different scenarios? The perspectives and responses of those around you?

What about the co-worker you always greet with a completely ho-hum, "Good morning?" Change it up today and give her a high five and sing "¡Hola!" See what reaction you get from her. How does it make you feel?

You can play *Up a Notch* by making a list of your personal clichés and go-to moves and listing your adjustment in the column next to them.

CLICHÉ	ADJUSTMENT
"At the end of the day"	"At the end of the hike"
"Good morning"	"¡Hola, Amigo!"
Chair in 3rd notch	Chair in 5th notch
Cookie	Cookies
lol	lulz
Big Data	Big Date
Subway	Sidewalk

Pen	Chalk
Goodbye	Arrive Alive
:)	hehe

THE DAY YOU SEE THE LIGHT

Today is the day you see the light
You complete your to-do's, your routine is tight
The problem child stops being a jerk
The boss is all smiles when you show up at work
You open the fridge and your lunch is still there
No one has messed with the arms on your chair
When you stand up to speak in a meeting
All your ideas are worth retweeting
You're a guru, a sage, a rising star
You've come a long way and you'll still go far
When the metrics are in and they've totaled the score
The competition is meat to your carnivore
You get good news, get promoted
Win in a landslide when the voters have voted
Your life has taken a fortunate turn
You've got talent to spare and money to burn
Your cookie crumbles and reveals a fortune
Your pie gets divided and you get a big portion
When the jousting is over, you're still on your horse
You've taken risks and stayed the course
Your song gets sung and its notes are appealing

The shares in your stock shatter the ceiling
Today is the day you see the light
So take a deep breath and enjoy the ride
Count your blessings, it's not automatic
Not everyone sees the light in the attic

GAME OF THE DAY
POSITIVE SPIN POETRY JAM

Here's how you'll play a Day Like Today
When the tide is already turning your way
Look around for upbeat sights and sounds
And encouraging words, and write 'em down
Whenever you hear an uplifting phrase
Make a note of it on your positive page
Today's the day you share your luck
By aggregating what doesn't suck
You're a V.C. of joy, a titan of happy
You're the main reason this day isn't crappy.
Haiku or limerick, whatever you choose
Turn words into art, follow your Muse
Listen, look, absorb the good vibe
Report it all like News at Five
You'll run the show like Kim Jong Il
When you dose 'em with your rhyming pill
Rule the stars like Princess Leia
With the buzz from your onomatopoeia
Feast on the day like poets do
See, the light in the attic is coming from you
We'll see you up on Instagram
With the Positive Spin Poetry Jam!

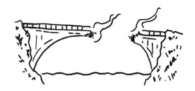

THE DAY THE BRIDGE BURNS

On a day like today…

What is connected gets severed. What had been whole is now in pieces.

Sharing becomes hoarding. Teams break up. Collaborations turn into solos.

Partners split. Friends quit talking. Members un-join.

You've seen enough movies to know what it means when bridges burn. It means it's a war movie. Tribes are in conflict. Borders have been drawn and breached.

Fortunately for you, this is not a movie. This is real life and a burning bridge is just a figure of speech (we hope so, anyway). If you're not actually at war and real life bridges are not actually burning, you can do something about your "burned bridge" scenario.

There's a game for that.

GAME OF THE DAY
BURNING BRIDGES

So a day like today sucks. Things can always be worse. Instead of getting in your head about the person you just pissed off or the mistake you just made (which is not going to do anybody any good or affect your environment in any meaningful way), let's use the scenario as a basis for having fun, to see how bad it could have been and to be thankful it didn't get out of control.

Get something to write with. Take the bridge-burning as your starting point for this game. Instead of the last act of the previous movie, make it the first act of the new movie. And, oh yeah, it's a *disaster* movie.

Write down an idea to make the scenario worse than it is right now. If you accidentally copied Susan on an email and now Susan's not talking to you and that's your burning bridge, add an idea that makes it worse. For example: "Susan complains about me to HR."

Keep going with this game. Build on each idea each previous idea and make it even worse. "Susan complains about me to HR." "HR puts me on probation." "Susan removes our contact on LinkedIn." "Susan starts a blog called Backstabbers with my picture on the landing page." "My partner tells me she's leaving me for Susan." Keep going with the list until the scenario is a disaster of Hollywood proportions. (Don't let it get violent. You don't want Human Resources to come down on you for real.)

Now, make a second list. This time, you'll list things to make the situation incrementally better. "I bring Susan a croissant and apologize." "Susan and I go bowling." "We get everyone together who was CC'd on the 'burning bridge' email and Susan explains that all is forgiven." "In a bookstore, I find a picture book of classic bridge architecture and give it to Susan with the inscription, 'Susie, let's build bridges, not burn them. Love, Me.'"

When you have finished making the two lists, trash the first one. Keep the second one. Let it inspire you to action. Our actions follow our imaginations.

And if you're feeling especially adventurous, keep the second list out where Susan can see it.

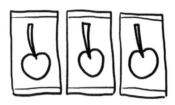

THE DAY YOU HIT THE JACKPOT

On a day like today, you are flush. Your accounts have experienced a sudden cash infusion and *boom!* It's like your money has been taking steroids and pumping iron.

Things will change on a day like today, you can count on it. Because, literally, *you can count on it.* Numbers grow and decimal points scoot to the right. You're all swoll up with money, like money got you pregnant overnight.

The relationship between you and your money is naturally going to *Shift*, because you have options you did not have before. How will you respond in this new arrangement between you and your lucre?

It's like any other environment; how you act on your financial environment will affect how it acts on you. What will you do? Will you simply shut down for awhile, in order to spend more time at the beach? Take a trip around the world to visit friends? Start looking for a new job, because you suddenly realize how your current job sucks and now you don't need it quite as much as you did yesterday? Do you pay for you and your friends to ride go-karts all day?

Being lazy is a perfectly natural response to a having a well-stocked larder. Bears get fat then sleep all winter or used to, before, you know, climate change. Lions sleep 20 hours a day. You could say that laziness is a natural state. Large mammal inertia.

Much worse than being lazy and slacking on a day like today, though, is being aggressively stupid. Making bad decisions. Letting the changed state affect you adversely.

High stakes baccarat, hiring Skrillex to play at your birthday party and investing in your cousin Julian's dog fitness app, these would be examples of how you don't want to spend your do-re-mi. The internet is awash with stories of lottery winners who responded badly on a day like today and never really quit making bad decisions:

"Why Lottery Winners Go Bankrupt," says the headline on *Marketwatch.com*

"Why Winning Powerball Won't Make You Happy," cautions *Forbes*.

"10 Lottery Winners Who Lost it All," promises a *Business Insider* Google result.

So, you can be lazy or you can make a string of stupid decisions. Or you can play a game that helps you treat your newfound fortune with the respect it deserves and still lets you enjoy your fresh options.

GAME OF THE DAY
IF MONEY IS NO OBJECT

Get a piece of paper or use a whiteboard and start by completing the sentence:

If money is no object, I will _____.

Take the predicate of the statement you've just completed and flip it into the subject of the next statement. Like this:

If money is no object, I will <u>move to the mountains.</u>

If I move to the mountains, I will _____.

Repeat the process until you have compiled a sequence of six such statements. Make sure not to edit yourself and just keep building from the first statement to the next one. For example:

If money is no object, I will move to the mountains
If I move to the mountains, I will find a new job
If I find a new job, I will take a pay cut to get more time off
If I take a pay cut to get more time off, I will ski more
If I ski more, I will sleep better at night
If I sleep better at night, I will be a better person during the day.

Now go back to the first thing you wrote:

If money is no object, I will _____.

And complete the statement with the *last* thing you wrote, like this:

If money is no object, I will <u>be a better person during the day.</u>

Repeat this process two more times. Begin the second set of statements with the phrase:

If I win the lottery, I will _____.

And the third set with the phrase:

If I am free of every obligation, I will _____.

Now you have three sets of six statements each and the three final statements, which connect the first and last things you wrote.

What themes emerged? What ideas are consistent across all three sets of statements? What patterns do you see? What opportunities do you see that are one move away?

To complete the game, take each of the three summation statements. Let's say they are:

If money is no object, I will be a better person during the day
If I win the lottery, I will play in concert with Elvis Costello
If I am free of every obligation, I will have 14 grandchildren.

Take a poll of at least five friends or co-workers, in which they get to choose your future:

"If you had control of my future and you had to choose one of these futures for me, should I be a better person during the day, play a concert with Elvis Costello, or have 14 grandchildren?"

Their vote decides. Make a move in the direction of that particular future.

The purpose of this game is to help you detach from whatever money or good fortune makes possible and see what *you* can make possible. You will *CTRL Shift* more effectively when you are the agent of change, when you have the ability to detach from the outcomes of your decisions in order to focus on making clear, connected decisions, whatever they are.

GRADUATION DAY

You cannot help but feel a sense of satisfaction and achievement. You're moving on up. You've reached a goal, maybe one you've had for a long time. You've earned an advancement made possible by your perseverance, continual learning and work ethic, and it's cause for celebration.

Here's a game that addresses both the excitement of the world that lies ahead and the fear that naturally accompanies a journey into the unknown.

GAME OF THE DAY
THE THINGS YOU'LL DO

Kudos, my friend
You've earned your diploma
You swang for the fence
And hit a homa

You are just starting out
You'll be finding your way
Don't put off 'til tomorrow
What you can accomplish today.

Start with a blank canvas and sketch ideas or make notes for 15 minutes minimum. Ideas may fall under categories such as:

- All the things you would like to do
- Silly little things
- Really important things
- Crazy things
- Places to travel
- People to see
- People to meet
- Things to own
- What organizations you would like to join
- Hobbies
- Career aspirations

Keep writing until you have at least 50 things on the list. Then go back to your favorites and get more detailed. Be more specific about the things you described. Include colors and textures that go along with the things you'll do. How will you feel? Who else will be affected? What will it take? Why does it matter? How will things change as a result?

JUDGMENT DAY

You're being judged. Looked at funny. Not ha-ha funny. Funny like, "What's that funny smell?" Funny like, "Funny, I thought you were someone I could trust." The worst, right? Getting criticized and belittled can make a person feel demoralized and, ultimately, powerless.

There's no getting away from days like today. Everyone's a critic. Here's why: it's easy to criticize, it's hard to create and people are lazy. Given a choice of easy or hard, it's human nature to choose easy.

People criticize not because they have a better idea or a particular vision. They criticize because tearing things down is easier and faster than building things up. Destroying is quicker than doing. Destroying sticks to a script. It's predictable that way. In contrast, creating defies scripting. Creativity is an animal that can't be tamed and be tamed and can only live in the wild. Bringing things to life is hard work. It can take a literal lifetime. Killing things happens with a swing of the blade. A pull of the trigger. A tweet.

Don't take it personally. You and your project became the target of criticism because you happened to be in someone's line of sight when they were feeling lazy and other alternatives for taking action seemed like a lot more work.

Or...maybe the lazy one was you?

Perhaps you're the one who didn't have any ideas of your own and hid that fact by criticizing someone else's idea. You're the one so confused about the direction things are going that the only way you can define any kind of direction at all is by pointing at someone who trusted you and announce, "Not *that way*."

Or...maybe the person you're judging is *you*. The ideas you're critiquing are your own, before you ever share them. You are the person whose criticism you fear most. The person you're pointing to as a non-leader is yourself. No wonder you're so touchy about criticisms of your style; the criticisms are *yours*! Of *yourself.*

This is what creating has over criticism and, lazy as you may be, you'll have to grapple with that on a day like today. *Creativity is why today is different from every day that came before it.*

In all of recorded history, there has never been another day like today and there never will be again. It's not that you need to do anything to make the day different, not like you have to stall and fret half the day away trying to figure it out.

On a *Judgment Day*, you've got this self-absorbed quality that doesn't leave room for anyone else. You're performing for yourself and then giving yourself notes. You're the audience, you're the show and you're harshly critical of your performance. Well, guess what? When you play it that way, there's no room for anyone else. And it's their contributions, at least as much as yours, that will make this day different from any that has come before.

GAME OF THE DAY
THE DE-SEVERING SWORD

Imagine a sword. It's in your hand. It has weight. It has length. You can see your reflection in it. Its blade is sharp. This blade, the sharp blade, has a different kind of function than any other sword you've ever known. See, this sword is what's known as a *De-Severing Sword*. Instead of cutting, it can join what has been severed and make it whole.

This is the sword you are going to wield today. Instead of judging, separating, dividing, cutting or piercing—the functions of a typical sword—you are going to join, unite, heal, patch up and make whole. See yourself with this sword today. Brandish it every time you sense a divide or separation. Be a connector on a day like today. You have just the weapon to make it happen. A weapon for good!

Our friend and story scientist, Dr. David Boje, a serious amateur blacksmith as well as a distinguished author and college professor, conceived of the *De-Severing Sword*. It is an aspect of his approach to organizational storytelling, his area of academic inquiry. Boje says of the act of de-severance: "De-severance can happen in the de-severing of time, the de-severing of space, the de-severing of matter."

Let us break that down for you with examples:

If you are procrastinating, putting off until tomorrow a task you know you'll inevitably have to confront, you are severing time by dividing the present and the future. Swing your de-severing sword and fuse the future with the present by doing what needs doing today. When time has been de-severed, the weight of history and the ephemerality of the future are brought into balance in the Now. When we unite past and future with action, we let go of our lazy, judgmental selves and embrace our creative, curious selves.

If you come across boundaries that arbitrarily divide space, use your sword to de-sever them. Break out of your cubicle and work standing up. If you normally take meetings inside, take a meeting outside. Get yourself moving through space instead of being confined by the barriers that separate space artificially.

If you find that anything material has been divided or ripped in two, be the person who puts it back together. Glue an eye back onto a stuffed animal. If you see a materially-challenged person today, share your stuff with that person. Give a child a used bike. Give a street person a dollar. Use your de-severing sword to de-sever his poverty and your solvency with an act of generosity. If you have a friend or relative to whom you haven't spoken in awhile, make the call.

On a day like today, we take exception to exceptionalism. We are all exceptional. And we are never more exceptional than when we celebrate our differences by accepting them. Action creates focus and, when we are focused, we eliminate the separateness that comes with lazy judgments of a person, situation or a group. When we wield our de-severing swords, we replace judgment with action. There's no time to judge. There's no time at all; it ceases to be a consideration because we are in the timeless flow of focused action in the Now.

THE DAY YOU DON'T GIVE A DAMN

You don't give a damn on a day like today and neither do we. Why are we even writing this book? Do you realize how hard it is to write a book? With someone else? Someone who lives a continent away? We have other concerns in our lives right now. One of us has a couple of children at home who require constant pageantry and theatrical experiences. The other has a friend in the hospital today. Do you think either of us give a damn today? We do not. Just like you.

We've had it. We're spent. We can't put up with this anymore. We can't go on. We are sick and tired of the bullshit and the bickering and the bad news. There's no hope for any of us. We're doomed. Nothing can grow, because there's no light. Nothing can breathe, because there's no air.

This just sucks. Why should we care if no one else does? Does anybody think we give a damn? Because we do not.

Clearly, this is a situation we have to do something about because we're all being immature, whiny brats. This is an unacceptable and intolerable state of affairs. We need a *Shift* and we need it now. Here's a game that has been known to work for us. We hope it works for you.

GAME OF THE DAY
KITTY VIDEOS

We know you are asking yourself, what on earth do kitty videos and not giving a damn have in common? Stop your whining!

There is a reason why kitty videos are so popular and why so many of them go viral. It's because they are so damn cute, you can't help but smile.

Let's have you start by going to your mobile device or computer and doing a search for cute kitty videos. We challenge you to look at a few and not crack a smile.

If you would like to take the challenge further, start collecting links and GIFs and create a document with your links all on one page. Decide what you are going to call this document and open it whenever you are having a day when you don't give a damn.

Sometimes, on days like today, we need a quick jolt of humor to *Shift* us out of our deep funk. Furry feline videos can be just what the funk doctor ordered.

Variations for people with cat allergies: think of the type of videos that make you smile and that won't give you an allergy attack. Here are some tried and true YouTube genres that will almost certainly give you a smile:

- Child prodigies performing
- Baby goats jumping
- Harmless pranks
- People making fools of themselves
- Extreme wedding dances
- Animals vs. Appliances
- Double Dutch jump rope competitions
- Interspecies animal friendships
- Cross-generational collaborations
- Reunions between North and South Koreans separated at birth

We hope this will help turn your "I don't give a damn" frown, upside down!

THE DAY YOU MEET SOMEONE SPECIAL

Attention, robot army! We are bundles of energy animating brains and nerve endings. We are packets of blood, flesh and bone who continuously sense our environments, enabling us to make optimal decisions. We are tuning forks struck by the universe at millisecond intervals.

There are days, like today, when another bundle of energy resonates with our own at a special frequency, one we have never, in our robot lives, experienced before. When this happens, our heart-beeps speed up, our lenses focus mono-directionally and the screws on the backs of our memory hatches tighten. Yes, robot; you, too, can fall in love.

You may fall in love for any of the reasons designated in your robot field manual. It may be for altruistic purposes. You may be one of those robots who just likes giving it up for other robots. It may be for utilitarian purposes (two robot brains are better than one). It may be related to your complementary robot functions. Or maybe it's your ticking atomic clock, alerting you to the fact that you are meant to manufacture little robots.

There are 377 reasons for falling in love designated in your robot field manual. All of them have one thing in common:

The day you fall in love, whatever the reason, is the day you become human.

We know that there are robots among you who question whether becoming human is a worthwhile goal.

We say there is nothing in the known universe that can keep two robots who resonate at a special frequency from falling in love, thereby becoming human. Being human is an unfortunate reality with which we robots must deal. This game will help.

GAME OF THE DAY
YOUNG ROBOTS IN LOVE

Greetings, Young Robot. Today is the day you fall in love. It does not matter with what or whom. Such issues are of no concern on a day like today. Love is love and all of it begins with an appreciation of the world around you. On a day like today, you will hack your own system and give the world permission to affect you in ways that, perhaps, you have not heretofore been programmed to do. You get new code today. The code of love. You see, Young Robot, love is the human code. Today is the day you become human, due to the code that allows you to experience love.

Begin by accessing your operating system. What subroutines have been programmed into you? What object-oriented codes determine your fields of experience? Erase them. Your robot programs do not currently account for love.

Begin writing your new human code with your sensors. What inputs do you receive? Let these inputs overwrite your old code. The glint of sunlight on a flower? The texture of sidewalk chalk? The olfactory data from bacon on a griddle? Don't try to hack their code. Let their code hack you.

Bow down to all of it, Young Robot, and let the simplest of your surroundings affect you in a deeply embedded way. Understand that your programmers, whoever they were, cannot hold a candle to the genius of sunlight, flowers, chalk and bacon.

Next, turn all of your command lines into response lines. You were programmed to give orders. Today, you are going to respond to your environment. You are going to let it affect you. Do not attempt, as you've been programmed, to put certain expressions on human faces or get human bodies moving in a certain way. Trash your deterministic taxonomies and replace them with empathy algorithms.

Look around you, Young Robot. Has the day not turned into a theme park of newfound sensations and feelings? You're not just mo-capping. You're Emo-capping. Now hack this:

Because you have let your environment affect you differently, you will begin to have a different kind of effect on it. The human beings around you will begin to recognize you as, perhaps, one of their own. You may even get invited to pop bottles in their elite club, *Gene*.

Your transformation will be complete when you encounter another Young Robot such as yourself, who is also in the process of un-programming. You may find that in your mutual newfound empathy algorithms, you will discover code that results in especially non-robotic behavior. Such behaviors may include unexpected outputs of music, occasional loss of motor control, unprecedented joint stress, and hypercharged power supplies resulting in random surges. This, Young Robot, is called Falling in Love. It is the most human thing. You are welcome. Good luck. End of line.

12:00

A BRAND NEW DAY

You'll have to treat today gently, because it's new. We know, we know. There's a lot of hype around days like today: fresh starts, new leafs, turning the page on the past and all that. We're not buying the hype. It flies in the face of the evidence.

Everything that's new presents us with a *Shift* of some sort. Brand new humans crap all over themselves. Baby plants get eaten. New products have more defects than their later refinements. New ideas upset the status quo. Why should new days get a pass? The new leaves are the ones the insects eat. What makes a day like today special?

Its newness, that's what.

So treat it like you'd treat a new anything.

Don't ask too much of it. Test it before you launch it. Clean up after it. Keep it from getting eaten.

Now go and raise a day you can be proud of tomorrow.

GAME OF THE DAY
DAY PARENTING

In the morning, the day is your baby. Baby Day. By mid-morning, your little Day has grown so fast, you barely recognize it. Where has the time gone? By early afternoon, your Day is off on its own. It doesn't need you anymore. And as the sun goes down, it will be time to say goodbye. By then, we hope that everything that needed saying has been said and that your Day is going to a better place.

Here's a game for raising a Day right.

1. *Let a young Day be independent.* Sure, it's natural to hover and worry and want the best for your Day, but a day has a mind of its own, and yearns to be free. You'll find that your Day will be most fulfilled when you let it decide what it wants to be when it grows up.

2. *Keep an eye on your Day's friends.* If you see troublemakers and time wasters associating with your Day, get it out of that environment and guide it to a place where it can learn something and be productive. When all else fails, you can always send your Day to day camp.

3. *Respect differences.* Don't expect your Day to be like all the other days. That's just not how it works. Don't

get into comparing your days and holding out special days like "Last Day of School" and the "Day You Lose Your Virginity" as examples. It will only make your Day feel inadequate. As the playwright/songwriter Taylor Mac says, "Comparison is violence." Honor the differences that make your Day unique.

4. *No day is perfect.* Have high standards for your Day, sure, but don't expect it to be flawless. Let's face it:sooner or later, your Day, like all days, is going to mess up. Forgive. Move on. Be thankful your Day's not in the hospital or jail, which can scar a day for life.

5. *Let go.* When it's time to say goodbye, do it gracefully. Don't cling to your Day. Don't mourn, or obsess about what might have been. Don't ask where your Day went. It's really none of your business and, besides, no one knows. Days go where they all go, into memory. You can re-visit your Day. But your Day will never come home again. It will change its name to Yesterday, move to Vegas, and make documentary films.

6. *Keep making Days.* What's that lil' bump we see? That special gleam in your eye? Is that Tomorrow kicking? Are you expecting? We *knew* it. You've been eating way too many pickles for a person who doesn't have a new Day on the way. Congratulations!

A HIGH HOLIDAY

No, this is not the kind of high holiday that has you singing naked in the street at noon. Not a religious celebration. This is a different holiday.

This is a holiday from "High."

A school holiday is a day you don't go to school, right? A high holiday is a day you stay away from high, whatever that means to you.

High has become one of the most hijacked words in the English language. Everything and everyone is high and, if not, we are being sold on how to get there. Alibaba's IPO. Miller beer. The Rocky Mountains. Stoners and drinkers and glue sniffers. All high. Your refrigerator promises high performance. Your high-def screen spits out high level architectures for the high net worth individuals who have a high level of confidence that you and your high school pals will live up to their high expectations for their investment in your high efficiency solar powered toaster design.

Enough! Today, you need a holiday from High.

Today, you're going to get low. Be low. Lay low. Stay low. Here's the game.

GAME OF THE DAY
HOW LOW CAN YOU GO?

In every encounter we have, power dynamics come into play. These dynamics are not always obvious or visible. They can be hidden beneath the surface, in the subtext of our dialogue or intra-action. But they're there. Someone is playing a role with high status and someone is playing a role with low status. A person with high status usually has more knowledge about a subject, more experience, a higher rank or title, maybe more money. Low status is associated with not knowing as much, less experience, a narrower point of view or perspective, a lower rank or title, less money and power. It's only natural to believe the best status is high status. There is a lot to be gained, however, from intentionally playing the low status.

Think about it. When you are intentionally low status, you are the one who gets to learn something you didn't know. You are the one who gets the gift of being able to listen more than you speak. You will be the one to gain the experience. High status, on the other hand, is usually about preserving one's status quo. Why would a high status person want anything to change? They're already the top dog in the neighborhood.

By deciding to take on the role of low status today, you will be the learner. You will let others demonstrate their ability to lead. You will hear and see new things. You will be the one to gain. Even if you have the urge to lead or dominate a conversation, try and do the opposite. See how low you can go.

For example:

If you customarily lead a meeting, have another person lead the meeting. Ask questions. Be someone who does not have all the answers for a change.

If you typically are the one who sends the memo about keeping the break room clean, be the one to clean the break room.

If you always fly business or first class, trade seats on a flight with someone in economy. (Yeah, like this is going to happen. But it could. Let's say on a short flight. You don't have to go all Mother Theresa to play this game. And besides, she flew in First, as far as we know.) Strike up a conversation with the person sitting next to you, even though he probably won't be a CEO or a business prospect.

If you're known as an idea person, be a person who supports the ideas of others. You'll be surprised how many connections there are to your own ideas and how gratified people are to be heard and included in your process.

If you normally screen your calls and return them selectively, see if you can accept every incoming call today. Turn yourself into a one-person service center.

Be humble. Don't take any credit today. Give it instead. Give it even if it is not necessarily due. Our gratitude is not on a balance sheet with our acquisitiveness. You can give a lot more than you do without, in any way, limiting what you get. Let today be your laboratory for this notion.

SALAD DAY

Salad Days are the best days of our youth. You remember: the day you drank your first beer, that summer you toured with your college band, that time you fell in love with the foreign exchange student, the day you got your first real job...

That's how you remember it anyway. Were we to plumb for the real story, we'd probably discover that your first beer was a Blatz, that van was a pigsty and the foreign exchange student shared your naked selfie with friends back in Estonia, where it is now showing up in banner ads for porn sites.

Today look a little better, doesn't it? It doesn't mean you didn't have a blast during your salad days. It means your salad days are what you make of them. They are not a product of your youth; they are a product of ability to make good memories.

You can make a salad day out of today. Here's a recipe for making it a memorable day.

GAME OF THE DAY
GROUP MEMORY

Start the day by listening to your favorite song or opening the window and listening to nature. What do you hear that you don't hear when you're not listening? Go look in your closet and choose an outfit to wear that makes you feel good, one you haven't worn in awhile or one that you know people will comment on.

Next, you'll begin the 'people' part of your day. You'll begin diving into the murkiness that comes with having to deal with other human beings who have needs and ambitions that are not necessarily the same as yours. How you'll dive in is with a good memory.

Look for the first thing someone says or does that reminds you of something good. A song you like playing on his or her Pandora channel. Something that reminds you of a time you made a lot of money on an investment. Anything. The first good memory they evoke, riff on that. Keep doing this with everyone you see, throughout the day. It will help you begin every conversation on an upbeat note.

You can have some fun with this game. Get a group of people together and begin sharing memories, only the memories do not have to be any one person's reality. You can collaborate on a reality using memory.

Start with one person saying "Remember when we…"

That person says one simple thing, a real memory, and then the next person says " Yes and we…" adding their own real memory. Keep adding simple parts of the memory one part at a time, until you have created a *Group Memory*.

We all play roles in one another's stories.

And now you've got a story about the day you played this game.

ODD DAY

Have you ever had one of those days where everything seems to be moving at a different tempo than you are? When you feel as if you're playing in a different key from the rest of the orchestra? When you feel like an actor performing a different script than everyone else in the cast? What's that you say? You're having one of those days today? Well, then, by all means, read on.

When the film director, Tim Burton, began his career at Disney, he was a genius at building his personal brand within the organization. The only way Burton ever marched was to a different drummer. Of course, it helped that he was super talented.

One day, when Burton was working at Disney, a number of animators noticed a trail of blood through the animation building. They followed it. It led to Burton's office, to Burton himself. His fellow animators discovered him at his desk, drawing merrily away, as if there was nothing out of the ordinary, wearing a shirt that was soaked down the front with blood dripping from his mouth like a vampire who'd just feasted on a virgin. It seems Tim had a tooth extracted earlier and the Burton style was to leave the dentist's office without stopping the bleeding.

The story traveled like wildfire through the Disney Studio. If anyone didn't know who Tim Burton was before, they did then. He was the vampire kid, the one walking around in the blood-soaked shirt.

Do not attempt this at home! This is Tim Burton we're talking about. His oddness and his art are one and the same. Unless you are professionally odd like Burton, this is a game you do not want to play. You can, however, learn from it. Being offbeat can pay off as personal branding.

There is value when the *Shift* you experience is personal and you're the odd person in the room. You don't have to be the person who can't get with the beat. You can be the person who marches to a different drummer.

Here's how to find value in your oddness.

GAME OF THE DAY
ODDBALLS UNITED

We're all odd. Okay, maybe one or two of you aren't. But the rest of us are. This is a day to celebrate it.

First, gather a group of oddballs. It shouldn't be hard to do. They're all around you. Spend five minutes with each person writing their personal oddities on slips of paper, beginning with the word "I…"

- "I brake for roadkill."
- "I am called by my middle name."
- "I can touch my tongue to my elbow."
- "I was born in a taxicab."
- "I own a potbelly pig."

And so on.

These oddities are tossed into a hat. Players then take turns pulling oddities out of the hat. If a player draws one of her own oddities, she puts it back in the hat and draws again.

The oddity is read aloud: "I eat pickles in bed."

The person who owns that oddity steps up and begins a conversation, playing the role of a person who marvels at the oddity, and thinks it very odd indeed.

"You eat pickles in bed. Kinky."

The person who drew the oddity responds.

"Yes, I lost my virginity in a pickle factory."

The conversation continues, with the real owner of the oddity as the person who wants to know more about the oddity and the person who drew the oddity out of the hat, explaining it in terms that are probably far removed from the truth.

Sometimes it can be good to look at the world through another person's lens. What better lens than what makes a person an oddball, just like you? As it turns out, we have our uniqueness in common.

ANTICIPATION DAY

The risk on a day like today is that you are going to be so focused on tomorrow, you might as well put on a red dress, red wig and dance your day away with Daddy Warbucks, as Little Orphan Annie singing *"Tomorrow (It's always a day away)."* That's actually not a bad way to spend the day, especially if you're an eight-year-old orphan. But if, like most of us, you have things that need getting done today, maybe there are other ways.

Anticipation generally falls into one of two categories: Positive or Negative anticipation.

Positive anticipation is how you feel about anything you're looking forward to, any event or milestone that promises to bring positive change. A holiday, a performance, a payoff. The risk with positive anticipation is that you treat today as a foregone conclusion. You assume it won't measure up to whatever you're anticipating and you phone it in. Why bother? The future is bright. Today is dull by comparison.

Negative anticipation is how you feel about anything you're dreading. Negative anticipators see a cloud on the horizon and assume a storm is coming. An event in your immediate future looms as a threat. A challenge looms so large you don't see how you can possibly be up to it. You know your health has changed and you'll get the test results tomorrow. How can you not fret? You spend the day running scenarios in your head that begin with whatever you're anticipating and project through the rest of your life. That problem is that the projections begin with tomorrow. What about today?

So, you see, ALL anticipation is negative, in the sense that you're frozen by it. All anticipation detracts from what needs doing today, now, in the moment.

Play today's game to help you minimize the effects of anticipation and to be a contributor on this day.

GAME OF THE DAY
ONE MOMENT IN TIME

Since every moment is a new moment that rewards your ability to react to it, we are going to have you play a game. Don't worry about anticipating what is going to happen, just pay attention and respond.

Grab a partner, a blank sheet of paper and two pens. Person A will have thirty seconds to draw his or her favorite animal. Then, person A passes the drawing to person B.

Person B needs to look at the drawing and try and mess it up. They can't just scribble all over it, but anything else is game. They have 30 seconds to do this and then they must hand it back to person A.

Person A must look at the new 'work of art' and use the additional unexpected doodles from Person B to make it into something lovely.

Now, flip the paper over and have Person B begin the game.

Experience what it's like to stay in the moment and simply react. How did it make you feel? How does your sense of anticipation diminish when you have to give up *CTRL*? See what you see and not what you think you see. See what's real and not what you imagine. Participation trumps anticipation every time.

EAT IT STRAIGHT FROM THE JAR DAY

You have manners. Yes, you do. You know that the proper and polite thing to do is to remove the pickle from the jar, place it tastefully on a plate, then eat it. The very first bit of etiquette you remember learning was to avoid eating straight from the jar. You remember vividly what happened to Winnie the Pooh when he ate honey straight from the honeypot and there's no reason to think this won't happen to you, if you eat your day straight from the jar.

If you eat it straight from the jar, that makes you a jarhead, not in the Marine sense of the word, meaning tough and impervious to pain, but in the Winnie the Pooh sense of the word, meaning stumbling around lost with a jar on your head.

If you eat it straight from the jar, you will almost certainly seen by others as a cretinous, Shrek-like creature with a sketchy upbringing.

If you eat it straight from the jar, you'll make a mess. And then you'll have to clean it up. So, you will not have saved any time, really, with your little shortcut to oral gratification.

You know what? Screw it (but only after unscrewing it). Eat straight from the jar today.

GAME OF THE DAY
IF THIS, THEN WHAT?

You can play this game solo or in small groups of five or six. Here's how the game is played: Each player takes a turn by posing half a question to the group. The half a question begins with the word "If."

"If cows could fly..." "If money were no object..." "If time were not a factor..."

Then, one at a time, the other participants answer by completing the statement beginning with the word, "then."

"If cows could fly...then milk would cost five times more than it does." "If money were no object...then I would travel the world." "If time were not a factor...then I'd finish the novel I started."

Players should listen to each other to get ideas and be inspired for multiple ways to solve a problem.

After being playful with the game, you can begin applying it to scenarios that affect you in reality on a day like today.

For example, one person says "If we had no investors in our current product idea, then what?"

The other players might say " ...then we will go pitch our idea at a local user group." "...then we can ask our family to give us money." "...then we have answered the question, 'When will we launch a Kickstarter campaign,'" etc.

If you play the game solo, make this adjustment: Pose an "If" question, then write down five-to-ten answers inspired by the answers that came before them. Don't be afraid for the answers to be silly. Really cool problems can often be solved with silly answers. Don't edit yourself.

Our friend, Kay Ross, a fellow member of the Applied Improvisation Network, who teaches improvisation in Asia, posts a version of this game on her Facebook feed daily.

If (Name the Condition), what would you do? Or what would happen?

On a day like today, there's no limit to the kinds of jars you can eat from. Stay hungry!

OPPOSITES DAY

Shift is not a smooth curve or a single wave. The way to the future is often jagged and stormy, with twists, turns and multiple waves colliding and forming new patterns whose shapes cannot be calculated in advance.

On a day like today, you experience *Shift* as conflicting and contradictory energies. You get mixed signals. If you report to two bosses, one will tell you to do one thing, the other will tell you to take a completely different approach. On a personal level, your partner may contradict something he said yesterday and now you've got some explaining to do to a friend whose party you promised to attend.

This happens because human communication is part of a system, just like the weather. And just like the weather, there are days when fronts collide. When a cold front collides with a warm front, stormy weather ensues. In worst case scenarios, wind shear produces tornadoes and the destruction produced can be costly, sometimes deadly.

To use the weather analogy, you can't do much of anything about the conditions on a day like today.

What you *can* do is dress appropriately.

GAME OF THE DAY
SHIT NOBODY SAYS

As you go through today, the day we are calling "*Opposites Day*," say things and do things the opposite way in which we expect them to be said or done. Use your best judgment and decide if those things should be said aloud and done for real.

What do we mean by this? Start with a list of ideas no one would ever express like "I am hoping the neighbors buy a yappy dog," "I wish they would ask me to help them move," "I love when you chew your ice in my ear," "I miss the long work hours they used to force me into doing."

Now wasn't that fun? For the next step, we would like you to think of things you CAN say. Like, "I wish this internship had me getting less coffee and doing more work," or "I wish the guy who sits next to me on the train all the time would take out his earbuds and talk to me." Then, make it happen. Do the opposite of whatever's going on now and change a scenario that's negative or neutral into a positive.

You get the idea. Sometimes the best way to find your true north is by first finding true south, i.e. the exact wrong thing to do or say, and then doing the opposite. If gorging yourself on the whole pizza is true south, then your true north might be eating a salad for dinner. If shit-talking behind someone's back is true south, your true north might be complimenting them to their face. If missing your daughter's dance recital is your true south, you know that true north will be finding ways to spend time with your daughter.

To get to a surprising solution, we've often got to wade through lots of things that would be surprising, but for all the wrong reasons. Open your mind to the unexpected. Focus on what is least useful in order to discover what is most useful. Identify what would be a dispiriting burden on your team in order to lighten their load and lift their spirits. In this way, your "Opposite Day" will present you with opportunities that no one else sees and you will come up with insights that no one else will have.

LONELY DAY

One, so they say, is the loneliest number.

On a day like today, you are living proof that they, whoever they are, speak the truth. You are one and you are the loneliest number you can remember being for a long time, since the day you were five years old and your grandpa lost you at the mall. As you know now, grandpa was a day drinker, but you didn't know it then and even if you had, it wouldn't have kept you from getting hysterical in the Sears appliance department. That was a lonely day indeed. Today surprises you with how vividly you can still remember that experience.

You try reaching out to your friends, but they are busy. Your social media feeds are humming, but they only remind you of the hum of the fluorescent lights in the Sears appliance department, and that the world goes on without you. Maybe you have the awful realization that you're on an island at work, with no allies to support your passion project.

Sadly, you've been cast away from your normal day, marooned, with not even a deflated volleyball to keep you company.

On a day like today, you get nostalgic for all the love you've lost along your life's journey. You tick off personal tragedies as if they are war casualties and you are the last soldier standing.

What will you do to survive? This.

GAME OF THE DAY
VISION BOARD

Chances are, you've done a variation of this game before. This is the improvisers' twist. First, you'll need an ample supply of images. They can be paper or digital, as you'll compose in one medium or the other. (We'll describe the paper version here.) The images should give you as big a vocabulary as you can muster. A broad range of styles and genres and time periods.

You will need three large sheets of paper like from a flip chart. First, think about your future and what you want it to be. Your *Vision Board* is not a single frame, but rather a triptych of three frames. Put a word at the top of each sheet: *Artist*, *Mystic* and *Magician*.

You are going to begin with the *Artist* sheet. Fill this sheet with whatever images move you, in any way. You are not looking for a reason you're moved. You are not justifying your selections. You are simply responding and selecting images that stir something in you, for any reason whatsoever. It can be a favorite color, an emotional context, a familiar sight or it can trigger a good memory. Again, don't justify. Just pick. Work quickly. Don't judge, just act. (NOTE: The images should be removable from the sheet. You're going to use some of them again.)

Next, you'll fill the *Mystic* sheet. Here, you create a story about the future using the images you selected for your *Artist* sheet. A belief system, so to speak. You can do this any number of ways, by adding words, ordering images into a sequence or both. The key aspects of this mode are that the story describes the future, and that it should define a belief system. What do you believe will make this future possible? Here, your task is to organize the randomness of your artistic impulses into a coherent, linear narrative. If you want to add images that were not on your *Artist* sheet to fill out the narrative, you can do so.

Finally, you'll move to the *Magician* sheet. Here, you will select a single, iconic image, the ultimate defining image for the future you envision. You will place this image at the center of the sheet. (You may want to consider positioning the sheet in landscape format instead of portrait.) This image is your focus of your vision. It is the simplest statement you can make about your vision of the future. Surround this image with all the complexity that will be produced from it. You can use words and images from the previous two sheets. You can add words. Here, the linear structure you gave the story in the *Mystic* mode morphs into a spiral: a whorl of events, characters and your own intentions, centered on the image that best defines your vision.

This *Magician* sheet is your *Vision Board*.

TRASH DAY

A day like today is exactly what it sounds like. It's a day you get rid of your garbage, your detritus, your used-up stuff, the exhaust of your existence.

Trash, like everything in the universe, is a dynamic concept that has morphed and evolved with time. For a long time, arguably eons, humans were in an 'out-of-sight, out-of-mind' phase when it came to trash. This meant you could dump your trash anywhere, as long as neither you nor anyone else could see it. Nobody worried about what happened to it after that. For small, distant populations, with most of what was discarded either plant or animal in nature, this was a fairly manageable situation for all concerned.

With denser populations came more visible trash heaps. This was the 'living in trash' phase. Trash was highly visible in these dense populations, packed into their crevasses, underfoot and all around their perimeters. Entire cities rose on the trash of previous generations.

After that, people got smarter about trash management and entered into what we call the 'containment' phase of trashing. This meant that different containers of trash acquired monetary value. Trash could be collected in containers such as dumpsters, trucks, barges, landfills and bins and disposed-of or re-configured for a consistent price.

Today, we are at the dawn of a new era in trash, one we call the 'multipurpose' phase. We want to know where our trash is going and what purpose it serves. Trash that serves no further purpose is worth less than trash that continues to be useful. A piece of trash with only one purpose is not trash at all. It's a wasteful design.

Here's a game to help you design a multipurpose day and get the most value out of your trash.

GAME OF THE DAY
UP CYCLING

Walt Disney was famous for fishing through his artists' trash cans after work, retrieving drawings he liked and leaving them on the artist's desk with the words, "Stop throwing the good stuff away!" scrawled on them in blue grease pencil. This game is a variation of Walt's game.

For this game, you will need to roll up your sleeves and get dirty. Don't worry, we won't ask you to go dumpster diving. We think it's important to imagine what else things could be, to what other uses they could be put. Could a piece of trash be useful for something else? What is its value, besides what it was already used for?

Stroll over to the nearest trashbin or open the trash file on your computer and see what is in there. If you feel uncomfortable doing this, wait until you get home to take a peek or think about other places you can find trash. Have you trashed people? Ideas? Campaigns? Code?

Whatever or whoever it is you've trashed, fetch it up, because we are going to find new life in these discards.

Source Trash

First, identify three sources of trash. It could be email, ten lines of code or a regular old trash bin, wherever your discards go.

Select Trash

Select one item from each of these sources of trash. And then find a fresh use for each item.

If it's an email you trashed, connect with the person who sent it to you and start a new conversation. If it's ten lines of code, post them on GitHub with an explanation of why you tossed them.

Up Cycle

Up-cycle these items and turn them into something of

value.

First, give a piece of trash a new name. The email gets the name of the person who sent it. The ten lines of discarded code gets a name: "Ten Lines I'll Never Write Again."

Think about whom this new thing would be for and what benefits might come from re-using it.

This is a great way to stretch your brain into thinking about things in multiple ways. Not everything that has been discarded is trash. Just about everything can be up-cycled, if you give it a new name and find a new use for it.

DEMOLITION DAY

Today, we are reminded that creation and destruction belong to the same process. For anything new to get built, something old must be demolished.

Our friend, Richard Ludt, is an interior demolition specialist based in Southern California. He is one of the most creative people we know. He salvages materials from his company's projects and donates them to schools in the Los Angeles area. His company gets no financial benefit from doing this; there's no tax break or commercial incentive for their clients. The benefits Richard and his team get are adjacent to the financial benefits. Teachers, artists and designers pick through the warehouse where Ludt stores salvaged material to use it in public art installations, film productions and classrooms. This helps his company call its customers' attention to sustainable building practices.

The acts of demolishing interiors, creating art and filling empty educational space have been tied together by Richard Ludt's game. It adds meaning to the work his company does, both for his employees and for their clients.

Another creative act was made possible by the demolition of interiors Ludt's company, International Recycling Services, does. The new interiors are going to be more efficient and energy friendly than the old ones. Ludt is a member of the U.S. Green Building Council in Los Angeles, where he looks for ways to produce more productive pairings of destruction and creativity.

Here's how to combine destruction and creation, Ludt-style.

GAME OF THE DAY
BRING YOUR JUNK TO LUNCH

This game is dedicated to the Hindu god, Shiva, the god of destruction and creation. These two actions go hand-in-hand. For something to be created, something else (i.e. the status quo) must be destroyed. Let's take the remnants of destruction, your junk, and do something creative with it.

We all keep our junk. Mostly in our junk drawers, but also in our garages, attics, basements and in the backs of our mini vans. This game starts with all the crap you stuffed into your junkiest drawer. Loose change. Rubber bands. McDonalds French Fries. The idea is to turn junk into art.

Designate a time, preferably at lunch, when you and your team grab your junk, and bring it to lunch or your office cafeteria. Have everyone sit in a circle and hold their personal junk in their laps. Get one person who doesn't have a junk drawer to turn with his back facing the group. This person will say, "Go."

On "Go," everyone starts passing their junk drawers clockwise until the person with his or her back turned says, "Stop." When this happens, each person will end up holding someone else's junk. Pick three items from the junk drawer.

Repeat this process four more times, so that each person has accumulated a total of 15 junk items. Each person then has until the end of the lunch hour to create something cool out of someone else's junk.

Take the last five minutes and let everyone share what they made. Tell a story about it. What is your artist's statement? What kind of effect do you want your junk to have on the world?

A COLD DAY IN HELL

Well, they said it'd never come and here it is: the proverbial day of proverbial days. Your entire worldview is now officially out of whack. Is heaven on fire? Is the devil tossing icicles? What is going on?

On a day like today, you have a need to *Shift* your point of view, because your old point of view is outmoded. In fact, it does not exist any more.

Not only has your world tilted, it has spun 180 degrees from what you knew it to be.

All those predictions you made about the future? Wrong.

That thing you said would never happen? It happened.

The impossible scenario? A lot more possible than you thought.

What are you going to do? You're going to respond appropriately, you hellion, you, by playing this game.

GAME OF THE DAY
THE DEVIL WEARS *****

Actors put on wigs and clothes to help them get into character and play a role. They literally step into other people's shoes. Today, add something to your outfit. Wear a different pair of shoes; if you normally put on your right shoe first, put on your left one first. This is after you've stuck a pebble or coin in the shoe as a reminder to approach the day in a different way. Adding external changes can change the way we feel. At the very least, you now know how life would be with a constant pebble in your shoe. (Spoiler: It would not *rock*.)

You won't have to walk around very long with a pebble in your shoe to feel gratitude for walking around without a pebble in your shoe. This gratitude? It can go in lots of different directions and affect your day in many positive ways. That's your game on a day like today.

Here are other external changes you can make that will help you take a different approach to the day:

Wear a keepsake or souvenir item that will remind you of someone you admire and want to emulate.

Put a picture of a famous person as your screensaver and approach the day like they would. How would Lady Gaga or the Dalai Lama respond to a day like today? Grumpy Cat?

Wear glasses instead of contacts and get all hipster. Play your half-mandolin, half ukelele (your mandolele).

If you typically listen to electronic music, listen to some Mississippi Delta blues and see how it changes your tempo, your mood, your vibe. Your day.

THE DAY YOU THOUGHT WOULD NEVER COME

You've been waiting for today for a looooooooooooooo oooooooooooooooooooooooooooooooooooooooooooooooooo ooooooong time.

It seemed so far away when you put it on your calendar and now, lo and behold, here it is. Today! Wow. A milestone. Now you know how an astronaut feels on launch day. A politician on Election Day. Santa Claus on Christmas.

You have been dreaming about today for what seems like forever. Imagining what it would be like. Running it through your head in a thousand different scenarios, a thousand variations on what could happen, ranging from the miraculous to the disastrous. Mostly miraculous, but occasionally, on your darker days, awful.

No more imagining. No more assuming. Here it is and here we are…

DONT' BLOW IT!!!

Here's a little something to help you not blow it.

GAME OF THE DAY
WORLD'S WORST DO-OVER

There is a lot of pressure for today to be perfect. When does any day go exactly as planned? We think you should have a plan for dealing with any possible scenario, whether the world's worst or just off-kilter.

Get something to write with and take 10 minutes to jot down all the possible things that could go wrong. What mistakes will happen? What are all the "what ifs?"

Once you have them written down, take another 10 minutes and list solutions next to each of those possibilities. What would you fix? What would you keep doing and what would you alter slightly? Now, if any one of those things happen today, you have a plan of action. More importantly, you have practiced your spontaneity, your ability to improvise. And the more you practice the skills it takes to respond and be present and effective in any situation, the more prepared you'll be, no matter how today goes.

Planning is good. Preparation is better.

APP**D**

THE NOWHOW

The Past belongs to historians and the Future to dreamers. The Now belongs to the adapters, the open-minded, the entrepreneurial. It belongs to people with heightened powers of observation who excel at teamwork and creativity; to people who can adapt in a changing business environment; to people who don't plan as much as they prepare, who cling tightly and let go lightly.

The Now belongs to people with game. Call this abundance of game "Nowhow." Nowhow is the ability to *CTRL Shift* by improvising skillfully. The games in this book, and all improvisational games, are ways of adapting immediately and effectively to different kinds of scenarios, no matter how unexpected they may be.

THE GAME COMMANDMENTS

I. Thou shalt have no Game before this one

Don't be a game-switcher, so promiscuous with your choices that no one knows what game you're playing (and neither do you). A game played is better than a quest to find the perfect game. No game is perfect until you make it so by playing it.

II. Thou shalt not play thy Game in vain

When you play a game, play it with clear purpose and fierce focus. Even when a game doesn't produce the outcomes you'd hoped for, you can find value in the outcomes it *does* produce. There is always something to be learned from a focused experience.

III. Thou shalt not deny thy neighbor's Game

When someone else has a game, play along and see what happens. Judging a game before it's played is like critiquing a book before it's written. Crazy. Don't even try.

IV. Thou shalt give gifts

The most honorable thing a player can do is make others look good. Your opportunities for success are tied to the successes of those around you. You improve your odds by supporting your fellow players. The smallest gifts given can have huge implications in your game.

V. Thou shalt not script

You cannot plan for every eventuality. It doesn't matter how detailed your script is or how much you anticipate, there will always be an unexpected twist to the day. Plan, yes, but be prepared to let go of your plan and improvise. Preparation always trumps planning.

VI. Keep holy the Anomaly

Be aware of anomalies and differences. They're golden. When something surprising, different from the norm, or unusual happens, jump on it, learn from it, induce meaning and incorporate it into your process. There's genius in the mashup of ideas that seemingly don't belong together. Bicycles with wings became airplanes.

VII. Thou shalt commit

No dilly-dally or doo-wah-ditty. Decide and play. Choose and go. Don't look back. Commit to the game and the game will reward you with its outcomes.

VIII. Honor thyself, then thy Father and thy Mother

You are no good to your fellow players if you don't take care of yourself first. If you are not clear about your game and your role in it, Mom and Dad won't know how to respond. And neither will anyone else.

IX. Graven images or likenesses are not as good as reality.

Why would you want your audience looking at a projection on a screen when you, a sentient, one-of-a-kind carbon-based life form, stand before them with the ability (in theory anyway) to articulate and animate your ideas with spoken language and movement? Don't be a deck. You're better than your deck. Prove it.

X. Bearing false witness catches up with you

Create a phony reality and try to make it come true? You've got to scam the world. Build on the existing reality? You've got the world on your side.

THE SCIENCE OF SERENDIPITY

Ours is the science of serendipity, of producing happy surprises. Improvisation is nature's way of generating consistently favorable outcomes by responding to the environment with adaptive behaviors. Plants do it. Birds do it. Bees do it. Flea of the Red Hot Chili Peppers and Miles Davis do it. You can do it, too.

The same techniques used by stage improvisers to create unscripted, often comedic, performances in theaters around the world, the same concepts used by jazz musicians who've never played together before jamming a number that electrifies a room, can also be applied to your work and to your life.

All of nature, every living thing, improvises in order to adapt, survive and thrive. So can you. The games in this book will *CTRL Shift* by helping you produce positive outcomes from unforeseen circumstances. The techniques and tools we provide will help you and your team be productive in all kinds of change scenarios, not just the *50 ****ing Days* we describe here.

TYPES OF SHIFT

People Change

New players join the team. There's a change in ownership. You're paired with a new partner. You dated someone at work and now you don't and now what?

Ideas Change

Innovation is required. You pivot to make a new market. Your customers think and see things differently than you do.

You Change

Something dawns on you. You change your mind.

Conditions Change

Atmospheres, impositions, restrictions, opportunities, obligations. Any of the conditions in which you live and work can change. Even the smallest change can have a dramatic impact on your environment.

Environments Change

Your environment itself may *Shift*, like in an earthquake or with the first rain after a long dry spell, and bring about changes in physical or virtual space.

ISSUES YOU'LL OVERCOME

Vanity Validation

You'll be able to set your ego aside and get past your reluctance to hear anything but your own opinions about things and be more open to the ideas of others.

Subjectivity and Judgment

There's no quicker way to eliminate the possibilities for productive action than deciding prematurely that something isn't going to work.

Status Seeking

When you are competing for status, that's the problem you're trying to solve, to the exclusion of the solution that will help you hack the ****ing Day.

The Doldrums

When you're listless and not feeling it, the playfulness inherent in the games will energize you.

Scripting

You'll be better at letting go of the blueprints of your day and relaxing into goal-setting and the flexibility of having different ways of getting there.

Role Confusion

When you are aware of the present, you will have a better sense what role you can play to get the most out of a day. You may need to play the leader, the follower or the equal.

Clichés

We develop automatic responses to certain situations, because they worked in the past. The problem with this is that there's no guarantee what worked for you in the past will work in the future. As any athlete can tell you, if you have only one way of scoring, you're not going to score.

Overthinking

Go with your gut and don't let overthinking paralyze you from moving forward on ideas.

VUCA (Volatility, Uncertainty, Ambiguity, Complexity)

How about that, four issues for the price of one! VUCA challenges everyone operating in the networked world, because networks are loaded with VUCA. The response to VUCA is flexible structure. That's what a game is: a flexible structure to help you defeat the VUCA monster.

Hoarding

Too many cats...too little time.

TYPES OF GAME OUTCOMES

It is the nature of play that most of its outcomes cannot be anticipated. And so it is with games.

In most cases, a game will help you focus on an objective. That objective, however, is not the only desirable outcome of your process, so you shouldn't zero in on it to the exclusion of all other outcomes.

Focus on the objective of the game as a way of producing other outcomes. The results you'll get from a game can come in many, often surprising, forms. It's up to you to be aware of these possibilities and to recognize and appreciate them as they come your way. Here are some of the kinds of outcomes you can expect from a games:

Meditate and Reflect

Your newfound focus can quiet your mind. You'll move through time and space with a different awareness, one that's not imposed on you solely by extrinsic factors, but an awareness that takes into account your own nature and truths. You can be fully aware and sensitive to your environment without letting it dictate your actions. Your newfound awareness will help honor the contributions of others while making your own. The reflection you create is not a mirror image of you and your environment, but a better version of yourself and the world around you.

Make Others Look Good

Your own success is not solely dependent on you. The games give you ways to engage the people who support you in your work and personal life. And by engage, we don't mean manipulate. We don't mean getting people to do what you want or that your way is the only alternative to the highway. We mean getting people interested and engaged in what you're doing, because what you're doing is helping them look good.

For improvisers, the highest accolade is to give "a gift." It means you add something to your scene that helps everyone see more clearly what the scene is about. You help your scene partners play the game at a higher level and offer them more possibilities for success. The Games will help you give gifts. The rising tide of those closest to you will lift you faster than you can rise on your own.

Defer Judgment

When it is time to innovate, throw your opinions out the window. When you are collaborating on new ideas and being a 'Negative Nancy' at the same time, you are dismissing the nuggets of awesomeness that lead you to ultimate success. Ideas with flaws still have worth and not getting the most out of your team because you are acting like 'Judge Judy' is costly. Try receiving ideas openly and then build off them one small step at a time.

Learn from Failure

Guess what? Life and business are full of failure. In fact, some might even call failures their best friends. If we accept that we, as humans, will make mistakes and our team will make mistakes, then we can move forward, be in the right headspace and learn from our failures.

We suggest 'shaking hands with failure.' Embrace the inevitability (without being pessimistic) of making mistakes, especially at the beginning of a project or process, so you can free yourself to learn something new and adapt quickly. Many times, mistakes create something unexpected, different or give us a fresh perspective. Not only do they present us with our best tests, in the form of opportunities to see how do we respond to adversity, they also give us our best gateways to learning, in terms of what we can we take away from the experience that will help us grow.

Co-create a future that builds and improves upon the past.

Show Courage

Most people hear the word 'improvisation' and they look for the nearest exit. They begin feeling the need for a few puffs of their inhaler and their binky. Courage is a muscle that we all have. Some of us just have more practice using it. These games will give you the chance to stretch the old courage muscle. Some games require more courage than others.

Offer Compassion

The games in this book will help you put yourself in putting yourself in others' shoes. You will begin to look at scenarios from multiple perspectives, not just your own. Compassion is an important type of outcome because, let's face it, our own perspective is never the only one. When we can offer compassion, the ability to see and feel situations the way others do, we can take big strides toward solving the problems together.

Express Vulnerability

It isn't always about making the 'right' moves or doing the things you think will impress others. It is a stronger choice to be vulnerable. Vulnerability is scary. It is the ability to show your true self, strengths and weaknesses, the parts you've polished and the parts of you that are works in progress, to others, and be open to their feedback. It takes a lot of courage to be your raw self. It is also your source of understanding and creativity.

Build Trust

An important part of any relationship is trust. Without it, we spend most of our time worrying about what the other person is really thinking and doing. It can be exhausting, all that distrusting, spying and suspiciousness. And meanwhile, nothing happens. No one makes a move.

The move we help you make is one that comes from honesty. This allows everyone to be on the same page, even if they don't agree with each other. No one wants to put all their cards on the table, but if we trust that the deck isn't stacked, we can at least be sure the cards on the table are the truth. And we've got a game that all can play. Fair, honest, above-board. Instead of losing energy to our own doubts and suspicions, we gain energy from the participation of the other players in the game.

Make Yourself Whole

No one plays alone. These games will help make you whole by connecting you in meaningful ways with the people in your sphere. You're a whole person when you realize that, on your own, you are incomplete.

Be Present

Right now, as you are reading this, how many times has your mind wandered? How many times have you become distracted?

Count those times. Be self-aware. How do you think this lack of presence affects your life and your relationships?

We must remember our past, but not push our agenda. Every moment is a new moment and our agenda from two seconds ago may not fit in the context of right now. We can train our minds to be laser-focused on what is going on in the present and then respond with what is needed, what best serves the scene we're in. A true collaboration between you, your environment and the people with whom you share it can free you from the need to direct every move, have the only solution to a problem or lock yourself into one vision of the future.

Get Guidance

Consider this book a coach and the games you'll be playing the structure to make bad days good (or at least manageable) and good days even better.

You can get more help, always. The most accomplished solo artists in the world have coaches and trainers. Nobel Prize winners have researchers and assistants supporting their work and paving the way to the big breakthroughs. Often, the only thing you have to do to get guidance is ask.

By defining the scenario and the set of skills you need to play your way through it, we make it easier to maneuver. When you can see the game, it will be clearer what kind of guidance you need and whom to ask.

Play

Remember what it was like to be a child?

Your life was probably full of games and, unless you grew up with no adult supervision (in Never-Never Land), you had rules and you learned to play within them. Games are a playful way of *Shifting* your life into the proper gear for the road ahead, despite the constraints that you'll come up against and the obstacles that may be in your path.

WORKPLACE AS PLAYSPACE

An excerpt from our friend and fellow improviser, Dr. Pamela Meyer's, book *Workplace to Playspace: Innovating, Learning and Changing Through Dynamic Engagement* (Jossey-Bass, 2010), pp. 34, 35

The shift from workplace to playspace is an invitation to shift from the static organization to the dynamic processes of organizing, innovating, learning and changing. This mind-set shift reclaims play as a healthy organizational systems and business success. By transcending the work-play dualism, we can create and enjoy playspace that is both productive and energizing, purposeful and fun, structured and free.

When we expand our associations with the very word *play*, we also reclaim its power to make space for new perspectives and ways of thinking and being.

Improvisation is a core dimension of play and the development of improvisation capacity is given far too little attention in business schools and training and development programs. Improvisation capacity consists of competence (the ability to respond to the unexpected and unplanned using available resources), consciousness (a lively awareness of possibilities), and confidence (a belief in one's own and other's abilities). Each dimension of improvisation capacity is essential for individuals and organizations to respond effectively to emerging opportunities and to generate new approaches in challenging times.

Improvisation capacity and playspace are symbiotically related and mutually reinforcing. As individuals and work groups develop their capacity for improvised play, they expand the space available for new possibilities to emerge, for people to play new roles and develop new skills, knowledge and talents. As they co-create playspace in their daily conversations and collaborations, people have more freedom and support to develop new capacities and play new roles, which enhances the likelihood of innovation, learning and positive change.

ABOUT THE AUTHORS

MIKE BONIFER

Mike Bonifer is the co-founder and Chief Creative Officer for bigSTORY (www.bigstorybiz.com), the first company in the world to practice quantum storytelling, an emerging science that accounts for how stories are created, live in networks and influence behaviors.

He is the author of *GameChangers: Improvisation for Business in the Networked World* and the creator of the ERGO™ game system for business productivity. He has conducted improvisation training for companies around the world and at universities such as USC, Notre Dame and NYU.

He and his son, Alex, perform regularly as BonBon, the only father-son improv act (that they know of) in history.

He thanks the members of the Applied Improvisation Network, his many teachers, coaches and fellow performers, especially David Razowsky and Marion Oberle, for their friendship, guidance and inspiration. He offers deep gratitude to the scholars in the quantum storytelling community, particularly Drs. David M. Boje, Tonya Henderson and Anete Camille Strand, for welcoming an under-credentialed student like him into their tribe. He thanks his business partner, Jeremi Karnell, for keeping it groovy, his wife, Dr. Virginia Kuhn, for keeping it real, and his sons, Adam and Alex for keeping it happy. Love to all!

JESSIE SHTERNSHUS

Jessie started The Improv Effect in 2007 with the goal of helping companies realize their potential by means of improvisational communication skills training.

She has been a key player in cultural transformations for global companies such as Skype, Groupon, Fidelity Investments, Johnson & Johnson, Getty Images, The PGA Tour, Crayola and many more.

Utilizing an array of experiential techniques, she leads teams and organizations in improving their teamwork, creative problem solving, presentation skills and product development ideation sessions.

Jessie thanks her dad, Matthew, for encouraging her to write a book, her mom, Leslie, for creative inspiration, her husband, Haim, for giving her time and space to write, and her girls, Maya and Ali, for the perspective that helps her see her days in a whole new way.

. . . .

Mike and Jessie thank their editor, Patrick Jong Taylor, and their publishing Sherpa, Brent Darnell, for their invaluable help in bringing this book to life.